Find Out About Ferrets:
The Complete Guide to Turning Your Ferret Into the Happiest, Best-Behaved and Healthiest Pet in the World!

By Colin Patterson

Find Out About Ferrets: The Complete Guide to Turning Your Ferret Into the Happiest, Best-Trained and Healthiest Pet in the World! by Colin Patterson

ISBN 978-1-84728-523-2

Disclaimer: This book is for informational and entertainment purposes only and should not be considered professional veterinary advice. If you have health questions about your ferrets, consult your veterinarian.

Praise for Find Out About Ferrets by Colin Patterson

"I owe my ferret Furball's life and my eternal gratitude to Colin Patterson for his Find Out About Ferrets guide. When Furball stopped eating for a week and became listless, I became hysterical as he kept losing weight. I cried over what could possibly be wrong with my little guy as he seemed to be slowly dying.

Then I came across Colin's guide during a web search, got it instantly and began poring through it to see if I could find out what was wrong.

It turns out that Furball's symptoms indicated he'd swallowed something he shouldn't have. Intestinal blockages are common for ferrets, since they have a bad habit of putting everything they can into their mouths, and Fuzzball loves to tear apart my socks and EAT them. The solution according to Colin is a type of laxative for ferrets. A visit to the vet confirmed that Colin was right. Now Furball is completely well again, and I feel so much better!

Needless to say, I feel Find Out About Ferrets is a must read for all ferret owners."

- Addie Van Zwoll
Kalamazoo, Michigan

"Hi Colin,

As a confused first-time ferret mama, your instructions were brand new to me, so I learned a lot. Now Slinky has stopped biting me. If it were not for your help, this ferret would have been back to the shelter."

- Lisa Molyneux
Montgomery, Alabama

"Colin,

I found your book full of terrific information that was helpful for me as a new ferret owner. Your book was comprehensive, well written and organized for easy reading. I'm a big animal lover and know quite a bit about many animals, however your book would be valuable for a first time ferret owner or someone who already has a ferret amd is looking for additional information on their care and behavior. Thanks for writing the book!"

- Gwen Edmunds
Albuquerque, NM

Contents

Why Ferrets Are So Wonderful: A Foreword by Ferret Rescuer David Boughen

Four years ago my life had hit a low I had suffered a serious stroke, divorced, the last of my nearest family had passed away, and my old friends had all died or moved away. I was alone and I considered a pet for companionship. I had to take into account my state of health, finances and where I lived, so cats and dogs were out and most of the usual pets as well.

Then I read a article in a local newspaper about a man named Richard who had suffered a similar life changing illness. Bored and fed up restricted to what he could do, his wife brought him ferret and a new interest was born. He took in more unwanted fuzzies and formed the East Coast Ferret Rescue and when I first met him he had about 156 fuzzies.

I asked him about me adopting one of them. We talked for ages and at the end he decided I would make a good ferret keeper.

"I have just the one that will be right for your first," he said, "but you do realize that you will be smitten and want more."

"No I will not just the one will do," I replied.

He then handed over to me a four year old jill named Allie and my heart just melted. He told me she had been badly abused and had to be taken from her owner. "She will need a lot of tender loving care and I am sure she will get it from you," he said.

My life began to change for the better from that day on.

All I had was a cardboard box for her to sleep in and a litter tray and how quickly she learned to use it amazed me. She never slept in any other thing and never knew a caged environment again. We bonded — with her sleeping when I slept, eating when I did and greeted me every morning as I came down stairs.

Months past and all was well until my birthday, when a women friend bought me a bottle of whiskey, so I had a drink. Allie came into the room and scrambled onto my lap as she always did, I held her and stroked and for no apparent reason to me she bit into the fleshy part of my right hand between the thumb and index finger. By God did it hurt and did it bleed and it was difficult to get her off.

So after several hours at the hospital I returned home. Allie was curled up in her box and I gave her a wide berth. Within a day everything was back to normal. And it stayed that way for months till I had another drink and exactly the same way she bit again but this time the left hand.

When I talked to Rik about this he told me more about the life she had endured kicked and stomped on when the owner came home drunk. She identified the smell of alcohol and with being hurt. I never drank near her again or handled her if I had.

Allie changed my life in many ways and lead me meet Carol the new love in my life.

One day Allie was in a very sorry state, fouling her self, dragging her little body when she did move and little pitiful cries as she did. I took her straight off to the vet. They gave her medicines and pain killers, but the vet could not tell me what was wrong with her. He suggested that I bring her the next day when his partner would be in surgery as he was more a specialist in ferrets.

So next morning I was there early. Also later that morning I was due to give a speech at the guild hall. The vet told me that the injury Allie had sustained over the years through that man's abuse had affected her nervous system and her bones had deteriorated.

I asked what could be done, and he told me he could give her pain killing injections every few days but she would still be in pain which would get progressively worse. The only other option was to put her to sleep.

He left the room while I thought about it. I held her and gently stroked her, she nuzzled and licked my cheek and my heart felt it was breaking. I didn't want to lose her. I loved her.

Every now and again she would squeal in pain then whimper as it subsided. I could not let her suffer so with that love I gave the vet permission to put her to sleep. I could not speak the words but the vet persisted as he needed to hear me say them.

I held Allie close to my mouth and made ferret chuntering noises as I did when we played and I said my good bye, as the needle went in she licked at a tear that had run down my cheek and then she was gone. The vet asked if I would like him to dispose of her body.

"No," I replied, "She is going home."

But I had to go and give my speech to around 200 people local government officials and important people. My speech was about the plight of homeless and alcoholics and drug addicts, and the charity I am representing that works to help these people turn their lives around.

As I spoke with some passion, I remembered Allie in the trunk of my car and my emotional control of my loss came to the surface, with a choked voice and bleary eyes I continued.

As I stepped from podium there wasn't a dry eye in the house and the applause was astounding. My hand was being shaken and patted on the back which was fine for it was my first ever speech. I was complimented on a very moving speech and how passionate I must feel about these unfortunate people. I could not admit that my tears and feelings were for my dead fuzzy friend.

The next day I drove 60 miles to the north Yorkshire moors to Allie's and my favorite place where we walked and played amongst the rocks, and that is where I buried her and where now I take all my furry friends.

David Boughen is a ferret lover living in the city of Hull situated on the banks of the river Humber on the east coast of England.

Introduction

I'd like to congratulate you for purchasing this guide. You've already done so much for your ferret.

You see, it's no small thing to take another living being into your home. Their whole world revolves around you. They eat, drink, and sleep based entirely on your permission and efforts. Their companionship comes from you, and their happiness is based on you.

In return from your little friend you too get happiness and unconditional love.

And the point of this book — what I hope to accomplish — is to make your life with your ferret as great as possible. Maybe your ferret bites, smells bad sometimes, or goes to the bathroom in the wrong areas. This book will give you the tools to fix all of that.

Additionally, this book will give you the tools to make your little one as healthy as can be, so they live as long as possible. You'll learn what foods are the most nourishing, what illnesses to watch out for (and what to about them), and how to create a positive, safe living environment for your fuzzball.

And finally, you're going to increase your understanding of your little one — you'll learn about everything from ferret body language to how they think... and by the end of the book you'll have a well-behaved ferret who even knows how to do a trick or two that will impress your friends.

Even if you're a total beginner and don't even own a ferret yet, that's okay. I wrote this book with the complete beginner in mind, so that with this book, you can avoid all of the misinformation and often-conflicting advice out there. *Find Out About Ferrets* distills everything down into practical info you can use right now. I try to skip as much fluff and filler as possible with this book, so that you'll be able to keep consulting back on it even many years from now.

So read on and apply all the steps you'll discover. You and your ferret will have the most wonderful life possible.

Chapter One: Ferreting Out the Truth

Despite the fact that ferrets are growing in popularity as pets, they still get a lot of bad press. Announce to a group of friends that you are thinking of sharing your home with a ferret, and you're bound to hear at least two or three stories of rabid, feral ferrets roaming the countryside and killing off wildlife.

Like most urban legends, however, the major concerns that people have about ferrets are rarely based on fact, but rather on the misconceptions that have been passed around for years by people without much personal knowledge of ferrets.

Let's take a look at some of the most commonly held misconceptions about ferrets:

Ferrets are wild animals.
Often confused with their wild relatives -- the black-footed ferrets -- people assume that *all* ferrets are wild animals.

It's just untrue. Ferrets are domestic pets that are meant to live with people just like cats and dogs. Their domestication isn't a recent event, either. People have been keeping these fuzzy creatures as pets in America for at least three hundred years.

Before they made their way to the US, there is evidence of people keeping domestic ferrets for the last two thousand years. As early as 400 BC, the ferret rears his fuzzy head in the works of Aristotle and Aristophanes. With this kind of history, it's surprising that anyone would still be questioning their status as domesticated pets.

Ferrets are usually infected with rabies.

This is another untruth. Living indoors with their people, and walking on a leash when outside, ferrets are no more likely to carry rabies than any other domestic animal.

In fact there has never been a case documented of a ferret passing along rabies to a person. There is a rabies vaccination that is approved for use on ferrets (see Chapter 11 for more info), and responsible ferret owners should have their ferrets vaccinated regularly.

Ferrets are rodents.

It's easy to see why this myth has been perpetuated. With their slinky bodies and small size, it is understandable that some people think ferrets are related to mice, rats and other rodents.

The truth is that ferts are not in the rodent family at all. They are in the mustelid family, making them more closely related to small mammals such as otters, weasels and polecats.

The smell of ferrets is so offensive no one will ever visit you again if you get one.

While ferrets do have a particular musky scent that is all their own, their odor is not usually unbearably distasteful to people. Fuzzies can give off a strong odor if frightened, sort of like a skunk but not quite so pungent. However, most of the ferrets kept as pets in North America have been descented.

If you are concerned with peoples' reactions to your fert's musky scent, regular bathing as long as it's done correctly can reduce the odor by over 90%. Check out Chapter 8 for the inside scoop on bathing your fert.

There are several other factors that can affect your ferret's odor. A poor diet is one contributor. Ensure your ferret is eating properly, and you will find a marked improvement in his scent (see Chapter 7 for advice on feeding your fert).

Unspayed and unneutered ferrets can also give off a more offensive odor than those who have been altered. There are a number of good reasons to spay or neuter your pet ferret, and a decreased odor is one of them. Chapter 11 has more information on the benefits of altering your fuzzy.

Finally, if you're concerned with your ferret's odor, be sure to work at getting him litter trained. Did you know your ferret can use a litter box as regularly as a cat? Once he has mastered litter training, be sure to clean his litter box regularly. Training him isn't as tough as it sounds. For training tips, check out Chapter 10.

Ferrets are ferocious animals.

A few isolated incidents of ferrets biting have been blown way out of proportion.

Like any animal, each ferret has his own temperament, way of dealing with perceived threats, and personality. Some ferrets are going to be more open to handling and petting than others. Some ferrets will run from a perceived threat, while another may feel the need to protect himself by biting.

When a ferret bites, children are very often on the receiving end. Very young children have a tendency to chase animals, get loud and excited around them, and corner them to try and handle them.

As with any pet, children should never be left unattended with a pet ferret. Leaving a child alone with a ferret creates a situation in which your ferret may feel the need to defend himself. For more information on introducing your fert to children, see Chapter 6.

Ferrets are a danger to area wildlife.
There seems to be some concern that because ferrets have an aptitude for escaping, eventually there will be roving bands of feral ferrets. The concern is that they will continue to reproduce -- creating more and more feral ferrets -- and that they will feast on all the wildlife in the area.

First, let's deal with the reproductive possibilities of the escapee ferrets. The majority of pet ferrets in this country have already been spayed or neutered. Therefore, a few ferrets roaming the neighborhood will eventually die without having produced any offspring.

Ferrets are carnivores, so left to their own devices in the wild, there is a chance that they may manage to capture and eat a few animals. However, given their size and lack of survival skills in the wild, a far more likely scenario is that ferts who escape from their homes will die from exposure to the elements or starvation.

Even if they managed to find adequate food and shelter, it is hard to imagine that they would escape being preyed upon by larger animals.

Let's face it, ferrets have been kept as pets for hundreds of years. If feral ferrets were a huge threat to wildlife, we would have seen much more evidence of this already. The truth is that cats allowed outdoors are far more of a hazard to wildlife than fuzzies.

Chapter Two: Are You Ready to Commit?

When you meet a ferret, you may find yourself completely charmed by his playful antics, cute appearance and sociable personality. Before you run right out to get one of your own, however, there are many things you should know about these captivating fuzzballs.

Bringing home a new pet is a big commitment, and should not be done on a whim. Adding a ferret to your home is no different. They have their good points and their not so good points, and you should acquaint yourself with all of a fuzzy's qualities before you bring one home.

The Upside

As anyone who has spent any time with ferrets knows, they can be wonderful companions. There are several reasons these cute little fuzzballs make wonderful pets:

- **They are sociable creatures** who can come to enjoy your company as much as you appreciate theirs. Ferts are fun-loving, smart and mischievous and can easily charm their way into your heart. With proper training and exercise, ferrets can become a welcome addition to your family.

- **They make great pets for apartments.** Fuzzies can make an ideal pet for you if your living quarters are tight. Many apartment dwellers have found that because of their size, and the fact that they are so quiet, ferrets make the perfect pet.

  They do a little bit of dooking (ferret-speak for "talking"), but unless they are in extreme distress, it's not usually loud enough to disturb your neighbors.

- **Your fur kid can usually adapt to your schedule.** Left to their own devices, they will happily sleep the day away. It's not abnormal for a ferret to sleep eighteen hours a day or more. Maybe your work hours are a bit too long for a dog who needs more attention and frequent potty breaks, but your ferret will be snoring the day away if you have a job that occasionally keeps you away from home for extended hours.

  Speaking of potty breaks, another reason ferrets make great pets is that...

- **They can be litter trained.** With a little effort on your part, ferrets can be trained to use a litter box, much the same way cats do. This helps keep the odor down, makes cleaning much easier, and allows you to feel comfortable giving your ferret plenty of exercise outside of the cage.

- **Most love going for walks.** If you enjoy being outdoors exploring, you may have met your match. With their curious natures, ferrets are natural explorers who will love to join you on regular walks (more on the proper equipment to take your fert for a walk in Chapter 5). These days, you can find harnesses made especially for ferrets in most pet stores.

One last reason that fuzzies can make excellent pets has to do with...

- **Their life expectancy.** The life expectancy of ferts is about seven years with some living up to twelve years. This means that your much loved friend will be around to share your life for quite awhile.

The Other Stuff

There is a downside to ferrets' mischievous personalities. Some of the habits that people can be less than charmed by include:

- **Stealing.** Commonly known as thieves, the word "ferret" is derived from

"Sure I stole it... but aren't I cute?"

the Latin word for "thief."

Ferrets come by this name naturally. If you leave one unattended in your home, you'll quickly learn how they earned the title. Ferts will steal any object that isn't nailed

down (and possibly even some of those, too!) and hide it.

At first glance, this may seem like one of their many endearing qualities, and I'll have to admit, it can be kind of cute. However, when you've given up an entire afternoon searching for something you need, only to find it's been stashed somewhere by your fun-loving furry friend, you may find this a less than appealing attribute.

- **High exercise requirements.** As much as ferrets enjoy their sleep, they love their playtime and exercise, too. This isn't necessarily a bad thing, but you need to be sure that you have at least two hours a day to give them attention and free time out of their cage.

Fuzzies who don't get enough stimulation in the form of play, exercise and interaction with you can become depressed, destructive and aggressive. If you don't have at least a few hours a day to devote to your fert, you should probably get a pet with fewer attention requirements.

If you are really concerned about your ferret's need for stimulation, consider getting two. They can make great companions for each other, and they'll have each other to play with long after you've called "uncle."

 A group of ferrets is called a *business* of ferrets -- sometimes spelled (believe it or not) "busyness" or even "bysnes."

- **Need spacious housing.** Although even people in small apartments have found living with a fert the perfect situation, they do need a spacious cage. The cage should be large enough to give them sufficient space to prance and play. It should also be large enough to leave extra room for their litter box. Make sure your ferret's cage is kept clear of items which they can pull into their cage and hide. More on what your fuzzy's housing requirements in Chapter 5.

- **Can be expensive.** Considering cages, toys, veterinary care, food and more, ferts are not inexpensive to keep. You will want to feed your ferret the best quality food to keep him healthy. You will also be replacing toys that get chewed or broken.

To be kept in perfect health, your pet ferret needs to visit a veterinarian at least once a year, possibly more often as he ages or in the case of illness, for health checks and vaccinations. Check out Chapter 11 for information on finding a veterinarian and the type of care your fuzzball will need.

Cages and litter boxes are usually a one time expense, but you will need to replenish litter and cage accessories fairly frequently. Be sure you can take on the expense of a ferret before you bring him home.

- **You'll need to ferret-proof.** Because these inquisitive fuzzbutts love to get into anything and everything, you shouldn't let them have the run of the house when you aren't there to supervise. Even when you are there, though, you may need to take some extra precautions to ensure the safety of your ferret. Remember, ferrets enjoy hiding things, digging and chewing.

  Anything of value to you which you would not want to be subjected to any of these things should be kept out of a ferret's reach. Chapter 5 reveals all you need to know about ferret-proofing your home.

- **Training.** As mentioned earlier, you need to plan on spending quite a bit of time with your ferret every day. This is important for his exercise, play and socialization needs, and it also ensures that your ferret receives all the necessary training.

  Like a puppy or a kitten, it feels good to a ferret to nip and use his teeth. It's up to you to train him not to use his teeth inappropriately.

  You also need to work on litter box training. Keeping track of your fuzzy's potty habits may not seem like the most fun you'll ever have, but it will definitely be worth it in the end.

If you don't put the time and effort into training your pet ferret, there's a good chance you'll end up with a pet who is more of a trial than a pleasure. Probably not what you envisioned when you first thought of bringing home one of these fuzzy little creatures (but I'll make it as painless as possible when I teach you about training in Chapters 9 and 10).

- **Allergies.** Something that may not be a problem for many people, but should be taken into account before getting a ferret... is allergies.

  Has your exposure to ferts been only from seeing them on television or spending very short periods of time with them? Do you tend to suffer from allergies? If you answered yes to these questions then you should definitely spend a little time with at least one ferret to make sure that you don't have an allergic reaction.

  There's nothing more heartbreaking than getting your home all ready for your new little bundle of fur and then having to return him because of the allergic reaction of someone in the household.

- **Escape artists.** Ferrets do have a bit of a reputation as escape artists. You will want to consider this, especially if you plan on taking your ferret out on walks. You'll need to make sure that he has a harness that fits properly to avoid losing him (see Chapter 5). You also want to get an identification tag to attach to your fert's harness while you are out. If he does manage to get away from you, this will increase the likelihood of him being returned.

- **Laws regarding ferrets.** Due to the misconceptions people have about ferrets there are a few states, cities and towns that have banned them completely or enacted laws pertaining to permits and licenses for them. It's vital that you find out how receptive your community is to pet ferrets.

  Some people might make the decision to get a fuzzy even if they are illegal in the area in which they live. Probably not a great idea. If ferrets are illegal in your area, chances are you'll have a tough time finding a veterinarian willing and able to give your fert proper medical care.

  Another possibility is you'll get caught with your illegal ferret. What happens then? You'll have to watch your beloved pet as he is confiscated and either sent to a shelter or humane society in an area more receptive to ferrets or, even worse, euthanized. Is it fair that some states and cities still view ferrets as wild, dangerous animals? Absolutely not. But you should still think long and hard before you bring a fuzzy home in one of these areas.

  Want to really make a difference? Lobby your state and local representatives to let them know what you think about their view of these lively, loveable creatures.

- **Long life expectancy.** One final consideration to keep in mind when thinking of getting a ferret is the one we mentioned in the pros column as well -- life expectancy. It's definitely good news that your ferret is going to be around for years to come, but it's equally important that you give a lot of thought to what your life will be like for the next decade, give or take a few years.

Now, no one can plan for every curve ball life throws their way, but there are many things we can take into consideration. Are you planning on moving in the next few years? If yes, are ferrets legal in the area you are planning to move to? Will you be able to find affordable housing that allows pets?

Are you planning to start a family in the next few years? Ferts are not always great with young children. You need to take the extra time and effort to make sure that your fuzzy is extremely well socialized with young children early on, or else maybe you should wait until your children are of an appropriate age to bring a fert into the family.

These are just a few of the eventualities of life. Take some time to think about how your life changes may affect your ability to take the best possible care of your ferret.

So... Should You or Shouldn't You?

Really invest some time thinking about the pros and cons of ferret ownership. For some people, they can make wonderful pets. If, however, any of the downsides of sharing your home with a fert have given you a twinge of unease, than wait. Do a little bit more research, and try to spend some time with some fuzzies.

Unfortunately, ferrets wind up being left in animal shelters all over the world every day because people jumped the gun without taking the time to consider the downside of sharing their home with a ferret.

 Taking extra time now to consider all the pros and cons of

sharing your life with a fert can save you and your ferret from a lot of stress, strain and unhappiness.

Now, if you've done your research, maybe even spent some time with ferrets at a friend's house or an animal shelter, and you still think that they are the ideal pet for you, then by all means, it's time to think about opening your home to one of these fun-loving little guys. If you're truly ready to make a commitment for the lifetime of your ferret, you are in for a wonderful adventure!

<u>Chapter 3: Meeting Your Match</u>

By now you have a fairly good idea of what to expect when you bring home a new ferret. You've considered the ups and downs, the good and the bad, and you still feel prepared for the joys and challenges of sharing your home and your life with one or more of these charming fuzzballs. Now we need to open up a whole new can of worms.

Just like people, each fert has his own quirks that make for a unique little individual. How do you find the perfect ferret to fit you and your lifestyle? In this chapter, you'll get an exclusive look at a number of factors that can help you meet your match.

Four crucial questions to ask yourself before you start your search for the ideal ferret:

1. How much time do you have to devote to your ferret each day?

2. Do you have any personal preferences when it comes to color?

3. Do you have any plans to breed your fuzzy?

4. Are there any particular personality traits you would like your new furry friend to have?

Once you've spent some time thinking about these questions, you have the beginning of your list of things to look for in a ferret. Let's consider in a bit more detail the factors that will help you to make the best decision when choosing your new fuzzy.

Colors and markings

For the most part, personal preference is the foremost consideration when it comes to the color of your ferret. Many people who share their lives with these master entertainers are partial to one color over another. However, color plays no part in personality. Whether you choose a sable, an albino or another color, you will be getting a lively, intelligent companion.

The most common color for ferrets is sable. These guys have coarse brown topcoats, or guard hairs, with a lighter undercoat. There are a few other variations of colors that fall into the sable category. Black sables have black guard hairs with a white undercoat. Chocolate ferrets have coats that fall somewhere on the line between milk and dark chocolate. They usually have a light or amber colored undercoat, and should always have a mask.

The next most common color for ferrets is albino. With many species of animals, albinism is linked with health problems. This is *not* the case with albino ferrets. Albinos, with their white fur, red eyes, and pink noses, were actually selectively bred. Originally used to help hunt rabbits, hunters preferred these white ferts with their distinctive colors because they were easy to see out in the field. Although with their coloring, albino ferrets may be a bit more sensitive to light, they have no more health problems than other ferrets.

Not to be confused with albinos, white ferrets have coats with white guard hairs, but they don't have the red eyes of the albino. These unique looking furballs have dark eyes.

A few other possibilities in ferret coloring include silver, champagne, and cinnamon. There are a wide variety of silvers. Ferrets that fall into this category can have just a few strands of light silver in their tail or be completely charcoal colored. They do not usually have a full mask, but may have a few spots of silver around their eyes.

There is some debate as to whether or not a true cinnamon red colored ferret still exists. The line between cinnamon and champagne has become a bit blurred. The champagne colored fert has tan guard hairs with a reddish tint.

 Diet can play a part in how red a champagne colored ferret gets, which is why champagne is sometimes mistaken for cinnamon.

As if the wide variety of colors they come in doesn't make them unique enough, ferrets also come in a wide variety of patterns. There are fine point and Siamese ferrets who have a light body color with darker points. Points are the legs and tail. These ferts have a "V"-shaped mask.

Roan ferrets have a mixture of white and darker guard hairs which evenly cover their bodies.

Then there are mitts. As the name implies, these guys look like they took a stroll through wet paint. They have dark bodies, but all four feet are white. They also have white bibs, markings which extend from their chin to their chest.

Some other ferrets with distinctive markings include pandas, who have a white head down to their shoulders and darker bodies, and blazes, who have a blaze of white reaching from the top of their heads down past their shoulders. This blaze pattern is also referred to as badger or shetland.

 Usually a ferret's coloring has no bearing on other attributes. There is one notable exception. A genetic link has been found between color and patterns and deafness in ferrets. Referred to as *Waardenburg syndrome*, this type of hearing impairment is most commonly found in blazes and pandas. For more information on training deaf ferrets, see chapter 10.

 Many people love ferrets with a mask. It's important to note that these masks do not fully appear until a ferret has reached adulthood. The mask may change a bit over time as your fuzzball ages, as well.

Male or Female?

As with choosing color, many people have a personal preference between males and females. Where personality is concerned, there is no notable difference in personalities between altered males and females. If you are considering an unaltered fuzzy, however, there are a few things you haven't thought of but should be aware of.

Males who have not been neutered, also called *hobs*, give off a much stronger odor than those who have been altered. When the unaltered male is looking to mate, he can become quite aggressive toward other ferrets.

If you're planning on keeping more than one ferret, you need to provide a separate cage for your hob when he is in his rutting, or mating, period.

Another consideration when sharing your home with an unaltered male is that he can become anxious, depressed and downright miserable if not given the opportunity to mate.

Unspayed female ferrets are referred to as *jills*. When a jill comes into heat, she experiences an increase in hormones causing her genitals to visibly swell. And here's the problem -- once a female goes into heat, she stays that way until she mates. The prolonged inflammation of the female's vulva can cause infection.

If the jill is not given the opportunity to mate, there is also a good chance she will develop a serious condition called aplastic anemia which is caused by a hormonal suppression of the bone marrow. This condition can be fatal.

 Although not common, jills can go into heat as early as four months of age.

Obviously, if you aren't planning on mating your ferrets (more about mating in Chapter 13), the best thing for everyone is to have your fuzzy friends spayed or neutered. However, having your ferret altered can be an expensive procedure. If cost is a consideration for you, getting a ferret who has already been spayed or neutered is probably your best bet.

 Once a male has been neutered he is referred to as a *gib*. A female who has been spayed is called a *sprite*.

The only other noteworthy difference between male and female ferts is their size. Males are considerably larger than females. Male ferrets are, on average, about 18 inches long, and weigh in at 2 to 5 pounds. Females, on the other hand, usually weigh 1 to 3 pounds and are about 15 inches long.

Not sure if you're looking at a male or a female? It's actually fairly easy to tell. Check out the belly of your ferret. Do you see something resembling a belly button? Congratulations -- it's a boy!

Age

There are benefits and drawbacks to sharing your home with either baby ferrets or adults. The question is, which is the best match for you?

Baby ferrets, known as *kits*, are undeniably cute. There's just something about a baby of any species that pulls at your heartstrings. It's important to remember, though, that your kit is going to grow into an adult fairly quickly. If you don't get him off to the right start, you may soon have an adult who is tough to live with.

Four questions to ask yourself before you bring home a kit:

1. **Do you have ample time to spend with your kit?** The care and training of your baby fuzzy is completely in your hands. You'll need to work on litter training and nip training (see chapter 10 for training tips), as well as giving your kit plenty of attention and handling to ensure proper socialization. It'll be well worth it to invest the time in the early months of your ferret's life.

2. **Do you have very young children in your home?** If so, kits may not make the best pets. Young ferrets nip much as puppies and kittens do. Their teeth can be tough on little fingers and hands.

3. **Is the kit you are considering at least eight weeks of age?** Babies should not be removed from their mothers earlier than this.

4. **Are you prepared to make a lifetime commitment to your new bundle of fuzz?** Bringing home a kit means that with proper care, and without other medical complications, you will be spending almost a decade with this lively creature. Be sure you are ready to make that kind of commitment before getting your new pet.

Adult ferrets can make wonderful pets, as well. The top 3 benefits of opening your home to an adult furball are:

1. **You could be saving a life.** Thousands upon thousands of ferrets end up in rescue shelters every year. Chances are the cute kits will be scooped up right away while the adults get passed over time and again. Opening your home and your heart to an adult can mean the difference between life and death, as many shelters have time limits on each animal's stay before they are euthanized.

2. **What you see is what you get.** Adults have fully formed personalities. Spend a little time with an adult, and you can get a good sense of whether or not your personalities mesh before you bring him home.

3. **Older ferrets have usually lived in a home already before they move in with you.** This means that someone else has already done the tough stuff. You can enjoy the benefits of someone else's hard work -- and take pleasure in living with a fert who has already been trained to use a litter box and not to nip.

Not to say that there aren't some drawbacks to bringing home an adult ferret. Bringing home a middle-aged or senior fuzzy means you'll get fewer years to spend with him. Also, like most of us as we get older, ferrets tend to get set in their ways. It will be tougher to break your adult fert of the bad habits that he's had years to cultivate than it might be with a kit.

Whether you decide on an adult ferret or a kit, one thing is for certain. You'll be entertained for hours by your new pet's silly antics and playfulness. Adults may not be quite as crazy as their teenage counterparts... but they still know how to have a good time.

Health

Deidre was sure she had found the perfect ferret. She saw him one day in the window of a pet store near her office. She spent close to an hour with him in the store before she brought him home.

Teddy, as she named him, was lively, outgoing, and affectionate. Her only concern was that he had a bit of a discharge from his eyes. As this was her first ferret, she asked one of the pet store employees about it. She was assured this was completely normal. It didn't take Teddy long to steal Deidre's heart. He charmed her with his entertaining antics and his fondness for cuddling up close to her.

After only a few short days, however, Deidre was alarmed to notice the discharge was getting worse, and Teddy was lethargic and had lost his appetite. She brought him to her veterinarian immediately. But it was too late. Four days after bringing him home, Deidre had lost her beloved little Teddy.

Bringing home a new pet with health problems can be a huge strain, both emotionally and financially. Most new ferret owners are challenged enough caring for their new ferts without throwing an illness into the mix. And there's nothing worse than giving your heart over to an adorable fuzzy, only to lose him soon after bringing him home.

Below are the 7 crucial rules to rate a potential new ferret's health before picking one out. Get any of these wrong and it can cause you a ton of heartache... and high vet bills... later on when unforeseen problems come up:

1. The ferret's coat should be clean and shiny with no noticeable hair loss.

2. There should be no discharge in the eyes or nose.

3. Fuzzballs should be alert, active and inquisitive when awake. Lethargy can be a sign of illness.

4. The fert should be up-to-date on all necessary vaccinations.

5. Ask about the ferret's appetite. Healthy fuzzies should be eating and drinking well.

6. Take note of how the ferret interacts with you and other people. Look for a ferret who is curious and interested in you rather than one who appears shy or aggressive.

7. Protect yourself by asking the breeder, shelter worker or pet store employee about health guarantees. Even a ferret who appears healthy can have health problems.

One, Two, or More?

Many people who are owned by ferrets find that they enjoy having more than one at a time. So should you get more than one ferret? That all depends on you.

The single fert can be perfectly happy with humans as his sole companion. Be sure you are providing him with enough playtime and attention, and you will have an extremely content fuzzy.

If, however, you are away from home for long hours, or if you simply would like the added entertainment of living in a multiple ferret household, consider getting more than one ferret. Your fuzzies can entertain each other and provide companionship when you aren't around.

There will be a little bit more cleaning involved as the number of ferrets you have grows, but for the most part, caring for two or three ferrets isn't much tougher than caring for one.

"I love you!"

One suggestion, if you're considering adding more than one fert to the household, is to bring home one at a time, and space the homecomings a few months apart. This will give you ample opportunity to train and bond with each ferret. For valuable need-to-know information on introducing a new ferret to one that you already have, check out Chapter Six.

Chapter 4: How Much Is That Ferret In the Window?

Now that you've figured out exactly what you're looking for in a furry companion, it's time to figure out where to find him or her.

There are several options to choose from. Ferret shelters or local animal rescue groups often have a number of fuzzies available for adoption. Some other options include pet stores, private breeders, and individual adoptions and purchases. Let's take a look at each of these options so you can discover what's best for you.

Rescues and Shelters

When a friend called Terry to tell her about a ferret at the local shelter who was in danger of being euthanized, Terry wasn't immediately enthusiastic about adopting an adult.

A seasoned ferret owner, Terry had been thinking about bringing home another fuzzball ever since her elderly ferret had passed away, but she usually purchased kits from a local breeder, preferring to raise them from babyhood. She was a little concerned about getting a second-hand ferret. Would she be able to bond the same way with an adult? Would her other ferts get along with a new, full-grown ferret?

When Terry's friend called a second time, however, and informed her that this was the ferret's last day before her time was up, Terry knew she had to help.

Driving home from the shelter with the three-year-old, sable ferret, Terry was thinking about her concerns again when she felt something on her leg. The ferret had managed to wriggle out of the carrier the shelter had sent her home in and immediately scooted over to curl up in Terry's lap! Terry was charmed by the ferret's trusting and affectionate nature.

The remainder of her doubts were laid to rest later that night when she found the new ferret curled into a ball napping contentedly with her other two fur kids. Terry renamed her new fuzzy Kismet, which means destiny, believing that fate truly took a hand in bringing this fuzzy into her life.

Every day hundreds of ferrets are dropped off at animal shelters. Some rescues and shelters take in only ferrets. Others take in all types of companion animals. There are some really wonderful fuzzballs at these shelters just waiting to get a second chance. Before you head off to the shelter, however, here's the inside details on what to expect...

- If you're interested in bringing home a kit, rescues may not be your best bet. Most of the ferts that wind up in shelters are teenagers or older.

- Usually rescues have staff members or volunteers who spend a great deal of time socializing the ferrets. This means you'll wind up with a fuzzball who is used to being handled, and there will also be people available to answer specific questions about a particular ferret.

- Be prepared to answer some questions or fill out an adoption application when you are looking to adopt. Rescuers have usually invested a lot of time, effort and love in the ferrets they bring in, and they want to make sure that you are ready, willing and able to give your new fuzzball the best possible home.

- Just because you are adopting, don't assume that the ferret will be free. Shelters usually ask for an adoption donation to cover the cost of caring for the ferrets, and also to ensure that you are able to handle the financial commitment involved in taking care of your fert.

- Usually a ferret will already be altered and vaccinated before being sent home from the shelter.

- You won't be on your own when you adopt a ferret. Many rescues and shelters offer you ongoing support even after you've taken your ferret home.

When considering adopting a ferret from a rescue or shelter, most people want to know why the ferrets ended up there in the first place. There are many reasons why people can't keep their ferrets, so this may be something worth considering before you take the ferret home. Many people did not do their homework before bringing home a ferret, and then dump them in the shelter when they realize that they are not just cute little balls of fur who can be admired through the bars of their cage.

However, others have legitimate reasons for giving up their fuzzballs. The four most common reasons ferrets end up in shelters are:

- Behavior problems the previous owner was unable to resolve (but maybe you can -- when you apply the secrets you'll learn in this guide).

- Owner's allergies.

- Moving to a new home that doesn't allow ferrets.

- A change in the owner's lifestyle, such as a job promotion or a new baby.

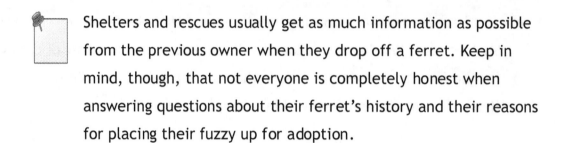

Shelters and rescues usually get as much information as possible from the previous owner when they drop off a ferret. Keep in mind, though, that not everyone is completely honest when answering questions about their ferret's history and their reasons for placing their fuzzy up for adoption.

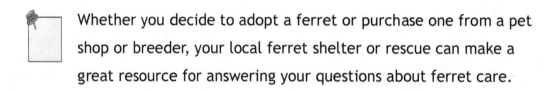

Whether you decide to adopt a ferret or purchase one from a pet shop or breeder, your local ferret shelter or rescue can make a great resource for answering your questions about ferret care.

Pet Stores

Pet stores are usually one of the first options people consider when they are ready to get a ferret. Most pet shops got their ferrets from mass breeders.

This is a controversial subject, because profit-making mass breeders tend not to keep their breeding ferrets under humane conditions -- and is that something you want to support?

It is beyond the scope of this guide to get into the ethics of mass breeding of ferrets, but what is not up for debate is that using mass producers means the pet stores will usually have kits for sale all year round, something smaller breeders and shelters cannot guarantee. These mass breeders tend to produce smaller ferrets than private breeders. This may or may not be a factor for you, but if size is an issue, be sure to ask a pet store employee where their ferrets came from before you make a purchase. (Some get them from local breeders or from shelters.)

Aside from ascertaining where the ferrets come from, there is a 6-step checklist of things you can do before purchasing your ferret from a pet store to ensure you're buying a healthy, well-socialized pet that isn't mistreated.

"Was I supposed to catch that?"
Photo by Dawn Landrum, Landrum Arts
http://LandrumArtsLA.com

- Make sure that the pet store is clean, especially the animals' cages.

- Do a visual check of the health of the ferret you are thinking of purchasing. (See Chapter 3 for more details on this.)

- Check with your local animal law enforcement agency to make sure no complaints have been filed against the store.

- Be sure that kits are handled regularly by staff to ensure proper socialization.

- Check to see if all ferrets are spayed or neutered and descented prior to being sold.

- Ask about the store's return policies, and make sure that they give you a health guarantee with your purchase. The health guarantee should be in writing.

 Remember, pet store employees are not often experts on all of the animals they sell. Make sure you do your homework *before* you get there, and don't rely on their word alone for information about the proper care of your ferret.

Breeders

Breeders can be a great place to get your ferret. They are enthusiastic about ferrets and their care. Their first concern isn't profit (and as many breeders will tell you, breeding is often *unprofitable* and just a way for them to defray costs), but instead about ferrets themselves. Small breeders also know the personalities of their individual ferrets and kits, so they can help you select the fuzzball that will best fit you and your lifestyle.

The disadvantage: since they're not factory farms, breeders may only have a few jills being bred at any given time, so they may not always have fuzzies readily available. It's not uncommon to be put on a waiting list to get your furball.

 Usually you will be purchasing a kit from a breeder, but they do occasionally have available adults who have been retired from breeding.

It's important that you find a reputable breeder. As with any profession there are a few crooks out there who are just in it for the money, and not interested in making the best match, treating ferrets humanely or making sure you have a healthy pet. Reputable breeders have a lot of love, time and money invested in their ferrets. They want to find the best possible homes for them.

How do you know if a breeder is a good one? There are 8 points that should tip you off right away. A reputable breeder will:

- Ask you lots of questions about the home you will be providing for one or more of her ferrets.

- Be more than happy to answer any and all of your questions.

- Allow you to see the living quarters of her ferrets.

- Be able to give you some information on each fuzzy's personality.

- Only sell kits who are old enough to be taken from their mother.

- Possibly be able to introduce you to the parents of the ferret you're interested in.

- Provide references from people who have purchased ferrets from them.

- Provide you with a health guarantee in writing.

It's not hard to find a breeder. You can start by doing an Internet search for ferret breeders in your area. Breeders may also advertise in the classified section of your local newspaper. The best way to find a breeder is by word of mouth. If you know someone who has a healthy fert with a great temperament, ask them to refer you to the breeder.

There has been a high occurrence of adrenal disease reported in ferrets who are altered prior to reaching sexual maturity. For this reason, some breeders may require you to sign a contract agreeing not to have your ferret spayed or neutered until they reach 6 months of age (more on health issues that can affect your ferret in Chapter 12).

Individual Purchases or Adoptions

Here's an inexpensive source of ferrets I guarantee you haven't thought of. You can even get a free cage, bowls, litter box and toys this way.

Sometimes when a person is unable to keep their ferrets, they will try to place them in new homes themselves. You can often find these ferrets by searching through the classified ads in your local paper or checking out bulletin boards at local pet shops or grocery stores. Also give your local vet clinic a call, since sometimes they adopt out ferrets whose owners are unable to keep them.

Obtaining a ferret in this manner has its good points and its bad points.

The advantage of getting a ferret from an owner looking to re-home him is that it is always less expensive as long as you do your homework. The owner may also offer to give you the cage, toys and other accessories as part of the purchase. Plus as someone who has lived with the fert for awhile, they can give you some information about personality, habits and training.

There are disadvantages to finding your ferret this way, as well. Individual owners probably won't provide any health guarantee for their ferrets. If they are trying to get rid of their ferret for behavior or temperament problems, they may not be forthcoming about those issues, hoping that they can unload their problem unto you.

There are a few steps you must take to protect yourself in this situation:

- Request copies of all the ferret's medical records.

- Call the veterinarian the owner used to make sure the ferret has been in for regular check-ups and vaccinations.

- Spend at least a few hours with the ferret before making the decision to purchase or adopt him to make sure he isn't aggressive, overly shy or lethargic.

Cost

Before you bring your new fuzzbutt home, be sure you've taken all the costs into consideration. The largest expense is going to be the initial expenditure for purchasing your ferret -- the cost of setting up his cage, toys, foods, vaccinations and other accessories.

How much should you expect to pay for your ferret? The amount will vary depending on where you live and where you get the fert. You should expect to pay anywhere from $75 up to around $250 if you get your fuzzy from a pet store or breeder. The adoption fees for shelters and rescues vary from place to place. Be sure to ask about the adoption fee up front.

The cost of setting your fur kid up in his new digs depends on how elaborate a home you make for him. On average, you can plan on spending at least $250 for an appropriate cage, toys, litter box, food and other accessories. The good news is that many of these things are one time expenses.

There will be some ongoing costs for keeping your fert happy and healthy. You'll be spending money on high quality food, new toys, and regular veterinary care. In some areas, you may be required to license your pet, as well.

 The cost of purchasing and caring for your ferret can run well over several hundred dollars a year. Make sure that all the necessities for taking the best possible care of your fuzzy are within your budget before bringing one of these fuzzballs home.

Health Guarantees

No matter where you get your new pet, the importance of getting a health guarantee cannot be stressed enough. There is nothing more devastating, both emotionally and financially, then bringing home a ferret only to find out that he has a serious illness.

With that in mind, you should be suspicious of any breeder or pet store who is not willing to give you a health guarantee in writing. If they absolutely refuse, you need to be aware that you are buying at your own risk.

I Found a Ferret... Now What?

It is possible that you may have a ferret who has been lost or abandoned by his owner show up on your front porch. If you find yourself in this situation, there are several things to keep in mind:

- Approach him with care. An abused, neglected, or lost animal will likely be terrified... and in his fear will be more likely to bite.

- You have no knowledge of the medical history of a stray ferret. Make a trip to the vet your top priority to make sure the fuzzy is healthy, free of parasites, altered and up-to-date on vaccinations.

- There may be a heartbroken owner out there looking for the fuzzball that landed on your doorstep. Check with local shelters and veterinarians' offices to see if anyone has been looking for the ferret. You can also place ads in the classified section of your local papers and hang flyers up in your neighborhood about the found ferret.

- If you are unable to give the lost little guy a home, there are many people who can. You can try to place him yourself by placing an ad in the newspaper, listing him on a site like petfinder.com, or placing him with a ferret shelter or rescue. Many municipal animal shelters take ferrets as well as other companion animals. You should check their intake and euthanasia policy before dropping him off.

 Think you've found a stray ferret? Stop! Weasels and minks can easily be mistaken for a ferret. Be sure that the animal you are about to rescue is indeed a pet and not a wild animal before you take him in. If you're unsure, call a local ferret rescue, wildlife rehabilitator, or your state's department of environmental management.

Chapter 5: Setting Up Housekeeping

You've found the perfect ferret. He is everything you have every hoped for in a fur kid and more. Now you're ready to bring him home. Or are you?

Have you...

- Gotten a carrier to make traveling in the car safe for your ferret?

- Picked out a spot in your home for your furball's cage?

- Gotten a comfortable cage roomy enough for your fert?

- Ferret-proofed the area your fuzzy will be playing in when out of his cage?

- Thought about whether or not you're going to take your ferret outside for walks?

- Found a veterinarian knowledgeable about ferret care?

If you answered *no* to any of these questions, there are still some preparations you need to make before you bring your ferret home. This chapter will help you with everything you need to make your ferret's homecoming a happy one.

Pet Carriers

Many shelters and pet stores will send you home with your new ferret in a cardboard carrier. Keep in mind that these carriers were not made with ferrets in mind. They may work for some animals like cats, but remember, you are about to bring home a cunning escape artist. The cardboard carriers are no match for your fuzzball's superior intellect and mischievous personality. It won't take long for your ferret to find his way out of the box and become a hazard while you are driving.

The same goes for harnesses, collars and leashes. These things are great for taking your ferret for a walk outside (more on this later in the chapter), but they are not appropriate restraints for your fert in the car. Don't let your first few minutes with your ferret come to a tragic end. Make sure you have your ferret safely in a carrier whenever you have him in the car.

There are a wide variety of pet carriers available at most pet supply stores. The best and safest for your ferret are the pet kennels made of hard plastic with metal doors. They can open either on the front or the top. Be sure that the latch is not something your ferret can manage to open on his own.

Think about how often you'll need to use your carrier, and how long your ferret will need to spend in it, before purchasing one. If you are only planning on the short trip home from the pet store and quick outings to and from the vet's office, you won't need anything too large. A small carrier with a towel or other comfy bedding on the bottom is suitable.

But if you're planning on taking your ferret with you when you travel, you want to use his carrier as his home away from home (more on traveling with your pet in chapter 8), in which case you'll want to invest in a larger carrier which can accommodate food and water bowls, a litter box, bedding and some play room.

<u>Location, Location, Location</u>

Now it's time to pick out the perfect spot in your home for your ferret's cage. There are 5 things to keep in mind when choosing the best place for your fert's home:

- **Avoid direct sunlight.** Your ferret may enjoy lying around and catching some noontime rays, but being left in the sun with no respite can be fatal to your fert. Be sure his cage offers plenty of shady spots where he can cool down on warm days.

- **Keep valuables out of reach.** Ferrets are fun-loving creatures who will steal anything they can get their paws on. Be sure they can't reach anything if they stick their hands out of the cage. This means knick-knacks, books, drapes, or anything else you don't want torn, shredded, ruined or hidden by your fuzzy.

- **Make sure the walls around the cage and the floor underneath it are surfaces that are *easily cleaned*.** Some ferrets are right on target when it comes to using their litter boxes while others may be a bit off. This means the walls around the litter area can become soiled.

  When it comes to playtime, ferrets are partying guys, and food and litter are nothing but confetti. They love digging and tossing these around so the walls and floor underneath the cage will probably need regular cleaning. A piece of linoleum underneath the cage and some Plexiglas around part of the cage can keep the mess to a minimum.

- **Avoid drafty, damp areas.** Basements are not usually a good place for your ferret's cage. You also want to avoid putting the cage too close to drafty windows, air conditioning vents or doors to the outside.

- **Keep in contact.** Ferrets are sociable creatures. Your fuzzball is going to be happiest in a spot where he can see his human family throughout the day.

 Ferrets are not outdoor pets. Although they may enjoy a stroll outside in nice weather, they can easily succumb to heatstroke in the summer and hypothermia in winter. To keep your fuzzy happy and healthy, keep him indoors.

Choosing a Cage

Below are 5 questions you must ask when picking out a cage. Get any of these wrong and your ferret will be too crammed in with not enough space... or bored with not enough to do... or even strangle himself.

- **How large is the cage?** *Spacious* is the word to keep in mind when considering a cage for your ferret. Think of all the things he'll be doing in this cage – sleeping, eating, using the litter box, playing. A hamster cage or an aquarium is not an option for your fuzzy.

  A good rule of thumb to keep in mind when choosing a cage for your fert is that each ferret should be in a cage that is at least 2 feet wide by 3 feet long, and at least 2 feet high. Of course, if your budget allows, your ferret would appreciate something even larger.

- **What is the cage made of?** Galvanized wire seems to be the top choice of ferret owners. It's safe and easy to clean. Avoid wood, as it absorbs urine and odors and can be chewed up by your ferret.

- **How far apart are the bars of the cage?** You better believe that your ferret will attempt to escape from his cage. Bars that are too far apart can give him just the opportunity he'll be looking for to squeeze through. The best case scenario is that your fuzzy will escape. A horrible possibility is that he'll get only part of the way through and strangle himself.

- **How accessible are all parts of the cage?** At one time or another, you will need to clean every nook and cranny of your fert's cage. Make sure that you find one that allows you easy access to all corners of the cage.

- **How many levels does the cage have?** More than one level means more opportunities for your ferret to exercise and more space to hang toys. The more levels your fuzzy's cage has, the more stimulation you can provide.

 Should you let your ferret live in your home without a cage? Some people keep their fuzzies this way, but it's not usually a great idea. Intelligent ferrets will get into things you may not have even thought about. For their safety, and the safety of the things in your home, you should probably leave your ferret in a cage when you aren't around to supervise.

Furnishing the Cage to Create Home Sweet Home

Once you've picked out a cage, you'll want to make sure you have all the accessories your ferret will need to stay happy and healthy. It'll be up to you to ensure that your ferret has a place to sleep, eat, play and use the potty.

Many of the best cages designed for ferrets have wire bottoms. You'll want to cover the bottom of the cage to protect your fert's feet. Linoleum, Plexiglas or carpet are all great materials to cover the bottom of the ferret's cage. Of course, whatever you choose to use, you'll need to make sure it can be easily cleaned.

Once you've covered the wire bottom of the cage, you can think about meeting your ferret's basic needs. First, since your fert will be spending a good part of his day napping, you'll want to consider his bedroom. Just like us, ferrets love to burrow into something soft and cozy to sleep. An old shirt, a towel, anything soft and comfortable will do the trick.

You can also check out a pet supply store to see the many creative items they have to help your fuzzball catch some zzzz's. There are hammocks, socks, sleeping sacks, tents and more to choose from. All of these things will provide your ferret with the perfect spot to curl up and snooze.

It's important that you habitually check your fuzzy's bedding to make sure that he's not tearing it up and eating it. Ingesting bedding can lead to intestinal blockage which can be fatal to your fert. Some ferrets prefer a bit of extra privacy at times, so a box or tent may be needed to make your fur kid completely comfortable.

 Unclean bedding is the number one reason people get the impression that ferrets smell. And the good news is that you can fix it in five minutes flat by putting it in the laundry. Be sure you wash your ferret's bedding regularly in order to help dispel this misconception.

Next, you'll need to provide a potty area for your ferret. Plan on putting your fuzzball's litter box on the lowest level of the cage. Ferrets are Olympic champions in the litter tossing category so keeping the box down low will minimize the mess.

There are a variety of litter boxes available to fit your ferret's cage, and you might need to try out a couple before finding the perfect one for your specific fert's potty habits. There are many with sides that are raised up higher than the front so as your ferret backs into a corner to go to the bathroom, he manages to still keep everything in the box. It's crucial that you secure the litter box to the cage so your ferret can't tip it over.

There are many types of litter on the market. How do you know which one is best for your ferret? Let's take a closer look at litter:

- Some of the best litters available for ferrets are pellet litters made of recycled newspapers or plant fibers, such as Yesterday's News brand. This type of litter is absorbent, helps control odor and doesn't create a lot of dust that your ferret will be breathing in. Best of all, it's earth-friendly.

- Shredded newspaper works well as litter. It's inexpensive, kind to the environment, and absorbent.

- Clay litters, like the kind many people use for their cats, is not a good choice for your ferret. Aside from being messy, it can create a great deal of dust which creates a real problem if your ferret inhales it.

- Clumping or scoopable litters have the same dust problem as clay litters. It also offers the added concern that if your ferret is wet when he enters the litter box (after a bath or playing in a water dish), this type of litter will stick to your fuzzy, creating a big lump of litter wherever it touches which will be difficult to clean off.

- Pine and cedar shavings are to be avoided. Despite the fact that they have been marketed as the best bedding for small pets for years, shavings have been known to cause serious health problems in several species.

 Ferrets won't usually travel too far to use their litter box. When they've got to go, any corner will do. For that reason, you'll want to keep an extra litter box handy for your fert's time outside of the cage.

Feeding time is another of your ferret's favorite times of the day. Make sure there is ample room in your fuzzy's cage for a food bowl and a water bottle. You may want to use a food bowl that can be secured to the cage, as your fert will consider bowls advertised as "untippable" a personal challenge.

Most ferrets also love digging and throwing their food around. The only answers to this are either to get used to it or try to find toys that will interest your ferret more than the food bowl. Getting used to it is probably the best bet. We'll talk more about the best food for your ferret in chapter 7.

 Keep food bowls out of corners, as corners are ferrets' favorite potty spots. Enough said.

The other things you'll need to add to your ferret's cage are toys, toys, and more toys. Your fuzzy will need some stimulation when you aren't there to entertain him, so a number of creative toys will go a long way in keeping your fuzzy happy and mentally healthy. Check out chapter 9 for more information on choosing toys for your ferret.

Ferret-Proofing

Ok, so you have a carrier, you picked out a spot for the cage and brought home the best, galvanized wire cage you could afford. You've decked it out with a litter box, food bowl, bedding and toys galore. Now you're ready to bring your ferret home, right?

Well, not quite. Your fuzzy is going to need plenty of time to exercise outside of his cage. It's up to you to make sure that the area of your home where your ferret will be roaming is as safe as possible. Go over your home with a fine tooth comb to find things that could mean trouble for your fert.

Once you've finished, do it again because chances are there's something you missed that your mischievous ferret will get into.

Here are 9 success tips to keep your ferret safe as he explores:

1. Plan on keeping your ferret out of rooms that have too many items that can be dangerous to him. Bathrooms, kitchens and laundry rooms often contain cleaning products, sharp objects, and many other things you don't want your ferret to get into. If you can't remove all of this stuff or make them completely inaccessible, then you should make these entire rooms off limits to your fuzzball. These rooms also usually have gaps between cabinets and appliances which your ferret could scoot behind.

2. Use high security baby gates or exercise pens to keep your ferret contained in one room or area. These should be at least three feet high or higher, or else your ferret will scale them.

3. Keep windows and doors closed when your fert is out and about. Your ferret can easily tear through screens and escape.

4. Furniture that your ferret can climb up into can pose a real danger, especially recliners and pull-out sofas. If your ferret gets into these he is in danger of getting caught in springs and clamps or sat on by someone who doesn't realize he's in the furniture.

5. Electrical wires and phone cords should be covered. Exposed wires can be chewed on by your ferret causing him to be electrocuted.

6. Intestinal blockages can be fatal to a ferret. Pick up anything that your fuzzy may chew on and ingest.

7. Put away anything your ferret will be able to pick up and carry off. Ferrets are treasure hoarders and will hide your valuables if given the chance.

8. Keep plants out of your ferret's reach. They can be poisonous, and even if they aren't your fert will most likely enjoy digging in the dirt and flinging it around.

9. When your ferret is out of his cage, everyone in the house will need to watch their step. Ferrets love to burrow and hide, making it easy for them to get stepped on or sat on. Make sure everyone in the house knows when your fuzzy is out playing.

Going Out on the Town

Although you shouldn't plan on keeping your ferret outdoors, he may enjoy a walk outside every now and then. If you're planning on taking your ferret out for walks, you must have a harness and leash before you bring him home. Purchase a harness designed especially for ferrets. Your ferret may escape if you choose something else.

 There are some collars designed for ferrets, but most ferrets can slip out of these if they are really determined. You're much better off sticking with a harness.

Pick a Veterinarian

You've gone to a lot of trouble to find the right ferret and set up your home to ensure he will have a long and comfortable life. Don't be caught unprepared for a medical emergency. Take the time to find a veterinarian before you bring your ferret home.

Most likely you won't need his services the day your ferret moves in, but if you do, you'll be happy you took the time to find someone who specializes in ferret care. For more information on finding a ferret vet, check out Chapter 11.

Chapter 6: Meeting the Family

The day has finally arrived. After all your hard work and careful preparation, it's time to bring your ferret home. All ferrets have unique personalities, which means some will feel like they've always been a part of the family from the first day they arrive, while others will need an adjustment period to get used to their new home and family.

There are six things you can do to help ease your fuzzy into his new environment:

- Keep your fuzzy safely in his own cage for the first few days. This will give him time to get acclimated to his surroundings without feeling completely overwhelmed.

- Keep noise to a minimum. Until your fert is used to your active family life, keep shrieking children, blaring radios and barking dogs from getting too close to his new home.

- For your fuzzy's first experience out of the cage, make sure he is in a quiet, safe area away from children and other pets. Take some time for your ferret to warm up to you, and then spend some time petting and handling him (more in chapter 8 on handling and picking up your ferret). If at any time it appears he feels uncomfortable, put him back in his cage and try again later.

- Once your fur kid is comfortable with being out of his cage and handled by you, it's time to introduce him to the rest of the family. Give him time to adjust to new people one at a time, introducing him to other pets and young children last.

- Use lots of healthy treats to help make each new experience a positive one for your fuzzy.

- Respect your fert's privacy. If he's burrowed under his bed or hanging out in any of his favorite hiding spots, don't yank him out and force socialization on him.

 Don't force your ferret to move beyond his comfort level before he's ready. Trust is an important part of the bond you're building with your new pet. A little patience on your part early on will ensure a strong relationship for years to come.

Once you're sure that your ferret is comfortable in his new surroundings and with all of the adults in the household, you can work on introducing him to other pets and children.

Ferret Meets Ferret

You may have a picture in your head of your new ferret and the ferret you already have catching sight of each other from across the room and running towards each other as if they just spotted the other half of themselves. The two ferrets will frolic and play and live together happily ever after.

It could happen. But it's also possible that, like most relationships, building a good one can take a little time and effort. Fortunately, using the method you're about to discover, you *can* introduce ferrets to each other without them harming or killing each other.

 First, a little word to the wise -- even if your new ferret adjusts quickly to his new household, keep him quarantined from your other ferrets for at least a few days. It's important you be *completely* sure your new fuzzball is healthy before introducing him to your other ferts.

There are 5 steps you can take *before* the introduction to make things go as smoothly as possible when the big event comes.

1. **Switch their bedding.** If your ferts want to snuggle into bed, they will have to do it in the bedding that smells like the other fuzzy. Because the scent of another ferret plays a big part in how they react to each other, this is a good way to have them get used to each other's smells before actually introducing them.

2. **Give everyone a bath using the same shampoo.** Again, this has to do with their sense of smell. Making sure everyone smells the same will even out the playing ground when it comes time to make introductions.

3. **Wash the cage in which you plan on keeping them.** Do a deep cleaning. Wash every nook and cranny in the cage, as well as toys and bedding. You should also consider putting a new litter pan in the cage.

4. **Prepare a neutral territory for your ferrets' first meeting.** A room that neither has been in before is ideal. Of course you should make sure it's completely ferret-proofed first (see Chapter 5 for more on ferret-

proofing). This will keep your ferts from feeling as if the other fuzzy is invading their territory before they get a chance to get to know one another. Another idea is to take them outside (on harness and leash, of course) to meet for the first time.

5. **Put your fuzzies' cages close to each other** so they can get used to each other before they have the opportunity to interact.

 Adult ferrets have been known to become aggressive about protecting young kits. They may try to hide them. They may also play too rough with the youngsters. It's often best to wait until your fert is old enough to hold his own with the adults before housing them together.

You need to supervise the first interactions between your ferrets. It's not uncommon for them to approach each other slowly with their tails puffed up. This is usually followed by some wrestling and roughhousing. You may even hear some squealing and hissing.

Give your ferrets a little time to work things out between themselves as long as they aren't doing any serious harm to one another. If at any time it seems like one of your ferts is really taking a beating or seems unduly distressed, separate them and give them a little time to recover. You can try introductions again later.

 If you haven't done it already, consider having your males neutered. Unaltered males are more likely to be aggressive, especially if you're attempting to introduce a new male.

Most ferrets will eventually work things out between themselves and spend many hours joyfully playing or napping together. It does occasionally happen that two ferts are just not destined to be together. They may always be agitated around one another. They may even fight and draw blood. If this is the case with your ferts, respect their differences, and allow these two to live happily apart.

Ferrets and Other Species

If you share your life with small pets such as hamsters, bunnies, lizards, or pet rats, it's a good idea to plan on keeping them separate from your ferret at all times. Remember, ferrets were originally bred to assist with hunting, so the movements of your small animals can cause your ferret's uncontrollable prey instincts to kick in.

Even if this is not the case for your ferret, his frisky style of play will probably be too much for your smaller pets. Rather than risk the injury or death of one of your pets, you're better off housing them apart from your ferret and giving them different playtimes outside of the cage.

Dogs and cats are a different matter. Dogs, cats and ferrets have been known to live together quite contentedly, but as with other introductions, getting your other pets used to your ferrets requires patience, time and acceptance of the fact that they may just never be compatible.

 Before trying to create a bond between your dog and your ferret, you should take your dog's breed and temperament into consideration. Just as ferrets may prey on smaller animals, certain breeds of dogs have high prey drives which may mean they won't make ideal companions for your ferrets.

You won't want to let your ferret and dog or cat out and give them a free-for-all for their first meeting. Fortunately I've developed a simple three step socialization technology that allows you to introduce your ferret to dogs and cats, easing them into a happy relationship using proximity, lowered barriers and play...

1. **Proximity.** First, while your ferret is in his cage, allow your dog or cat into the room. You may want to do this for several days or more before moving on. This allows your pets to get used to each other's strange smells, noises, and movements with the safety of the bars of the cage between them.

2. **Lowered Barriers.** Once your pets seem comfortable being in the same room, you can start introducing them outside of the cage. You can hold your cat on your lap or your dog on a leash while another family member brings the ferret over.

   Try to make this meeting as positive as possible with lots of encouragement and praise for good behavior. Don't use treats, as competition over food can lead to some problems. Let your pets sniff and get a feel for each other. Keep this first meeting brief so it ends on a positive (or at least not a negative) note. Increase the amount of time your pets are exposed to each other each time you have them meet.

3. **Mutual Play.** Once your pets seem comfortable with each other, you can let them play together on the floor. Be super vigilant. A large dog can hurt a ferret pretty easily, even if it is unintentional. A playful nip from your fert can be misinterpreted as aggression by your cat. Again, keep the first play session short and positive, and work your way up to longer play dates.

Don't force a relationship. If your pets don't get along then you need to be accepting of the fact that they may never be the best of friends.

The most important thing to remember is that you should *never* leave your ferrets unsupervised with other pets, even if your ferret is in his cage.

 Stay aware of your body language when you introduce your pets. Animals are very perceptive, and if you are tense or overly cautious, they may pick up on it, and react accordingly.

 If you have several other pets, introduce each one individually to your fuzzy. Too may at once may seem overwhelming to your fert, and you won't have as much control over the situation. Also, all animals have unique temperaments. Your ferret may get along well with one of your pets and not at all with another.

Ferrets and Children

The topic of children and animals is a tough one. There are a ton of stories, movies and works of art devoted to the idyllic relationship between children and animals. Yet quite often when an animal bites, it's a child on the receiving end. There are several reasons for this, many of them preventable. In this section we'll discuss how to keep your child and your ferret safe.

The truth is that very young children and ferrets do not make the best match. Toddlers and preschoolers have a tendency to squeeze their pets tightly when they hug them, pull on tails and ears, and try to play with them when all the animal wants is a nap.

You know your child is not being malicious or attempting to harm your ferret when she plays with him. Unfortunately, your ferret does not have this same awareness. If a young child plays too roughly, your fert may be put into a situation in which he feels the need to defend himself.

This is a problem that works both ways. Ferrets like to roughhouse when they play. Young ferrets and those who have not received training have a tendency to nip, and a ferret's long claws can scratch. Even though it's unintentional, a small child can easily be hurt when playing with a ferret.

The older your child, the more capable she is of understanding instructions for handling and playing with your fuzzball. In this case, you can introduce your fert to your child in much the same way you got him used to being handled by you and other adult family members.

Start by having your child interact with your ferret when he is still in his cage. She can drop treats and speak to him softly. When your fert seems comfortable, have your child sit quietly on the floor and let your ferret out of his cage. Allow your fuzzy to approach and move away as he wishes. Once the ferret is comfortable, spend time showing your child the proper way to handle the ferret.

If the ferret becomes uncomfortable or too hyper for your child, or if your child becomes too excited around your fert, stop the play session and try again at another time.

 This cannot be stressed enough. Children should *never* be left unsupervised with a ferret (or any other pet) no matter how comfortable they seem to be together. This is asking for trouble, and putting both your child and your fuzzball at risk.

Here are the 7 secrets to making the relationship between your child and ferret a good one:

1. Wait until your child is old enough to understand and follow rules about handling your ferret before you bring one home.

2. If having young children and ferts in the house at the same time is unavoidable, never leave them alone together, even if your fuzzy is in his cage.

3. If the fuzzy comes into your life before the kids, be sure he is well socialized to children so he won't be completely overwhelmed when you bring a new baby home.

4. Adopt an adult rather than a kit. An adult is less likely to nip. Also, if you go to a rescue, they may be able to find an adult fuzzy who has lived harmoniously with children already.

5. Be very clear with the rules governing your child's interaction with your fert *before* she handles him. Let her know the consequences of breaking these rules (e.g., not being allowed to play with the ferret for awhile, not getting to participate in an activity she enjoys) and stick with it.

6. Allow your child to help you in the day-to-day care of your fuzzy. Assign your child age appropriate chores, such as filling the water bowl, cleaning the litter box, etc.

7. Something that may come up with your children once you bring a ferret into the family is the desire to show him off to all of their friends. Make some rules beforehand on how to handle this. The parents of your

children's friends should be consulted before any interaction occurs.

It *is* possible for children and ferrets to live together happily. The key to making this relationship work is adult supervision at all times.

Chapter 7: Fuzzy Cuisine

No matter what you feed your little ones, when choosing the best food for your ferret, there are 4 unbreakable rules of what you must look for in food labels. I use the acronym FFAT (Fat, Fiber, Animal and Taurine):

1. **High in *Fat*.** 20% of your fuzzy's calories should come from fat.

2. **Low in *Fiber*.** Ferrets are unable to digest plant matter. Foods that are too high in fiber offer little or no nutritional value to your ferret, as they can not be digested.

3. **High in *Animal* protein.** Ferrets are carnivores, so 34-36% of their diet should come from animal proteins. When you check out the food label, you should look for meat or meat meals in the ingredient list. Stay away from meat-by-products.

4. **High in *Taurine*.** This nutrient is vital in keeping your fert's heart healthy and vision acute.

 If you are concerned about whether or not the food you are feeding your ferret is giving him everything he needs to stay healthy, consult your veterinarian or an expert in ferret care. Avoid asking the staff at pet stores, as not all of them are experts in ferret care, and may give incorrect information.

All Foods Are Not Created Equal

People feed their fuzzballs a variety of diets from specially formulated ferret foods to cat food to table scraps. Not all of these are good for your pets. We just mentioned the FFAT components that are vital in keeping your fert happy and healthy. Where can you find foods that contain all of the things your ferret needs with none of the stuff he doesn't? Let's look at the options:

- **Ferret food:** Other than raw foods (which we'll get to in a second), this is usually your safest bet. These foods are formulated with your ferret's unique nutritional needs in mind. Look for ferret kibble that doesn't contain much filler, such as grains or meat by-products. These may cost a bit more than other foods, but they are the best for your fert.

- **Cat food:** If you're considering feeding your ferret cat food, stick with dry kitten food. This should be high in protein and fat, as well as contain taurine. Again, make sure there aren't unhealthy filler ingredients like corn, by-products, etc.

- **Dog food:** Rover's food does not meet the minimum nutritional requirements for your fert.

- **Table scraps:** Although a few table scraps given as treats here and there won't hurt your fuzzy, they should definitely not be the mainstay of your ferret's diet (more later in this chapter on treats). Too many table scraps can cause digestive problems and blockages, diarrhea, and malnutrition.

It's important that you feed a high quality food with as little filler as possible. If you use a food that contains extra ingredients that don't meet your fert's nutritional needs, you may find he is eating more calories than he needs in an attempt to fulfill his nutritional requirements. This can lead to obesity which in turn can lead to other health problems. So remember: to avoid him becoming fat, feed your ferret FFAT.

Raw Food Diets

There is a controversial alternative to feeding your fert commercial ferret or kitten food, and before I get into it, I must warn you to consult your veterinarian before making any dietary decisions regarding your ferret.

Many people are turning to a natural, raw food diet for their ferrets. This involves feeding your fuzzy meat and bones to provide him with adequate nutrition without fillers such as carbohydrates.

Although there has not been much research on the effect of raw food diets in regard to ferrets, we have seen many notable benefits of this type of diet in other species including dogs, cats, rabbits, and birds. Plus, anecdotally, people who switch their ferrets to raw food are reporting that it doubles their fuzzy's lifespan -- often to 12 years and even as high as 15!

Specific benefits of this type of diet include:

- Decrease in gastrointestinal disease.

- Loss of excess weight.

- Increase in energy level (okay, you may not see this one as a benefit when your fuzzy is already bouncing off the walls).

- Lower incidence of premature death.

- Decrease in coat and skin problems.

 One benefit that scientific researchers recently noted in ferts who are fed a natural diet is that they seem to have a lower incidence of insulinoma, a cancer common in ferrets.

There are two types of raw food diet that you can feed your fert, a whole prey diet or a raw carnivore diet. Let's take a closer look at these two options:

Whole prey diet: The more extreme (and controversial) of the two, this is exactly what it sounds like. With this type of diet, you'll be feeding your fert whole animals, either alive or frozen. Foods include animals such as mice, chicks and rats.

Many experts believe whole prey is the ideal ferret diet for four reasons:

1. It is easy for your fuzzy to digest with no added plant matter.

2. Chewing the meat and bones helps keep your fert's gums and teeth clean and healthy.

3. If you feed live animals, chasing, tearing and chewing whole animals provides excellent mental stimulation for your fuzzball.

4. Your fuzzy will probably be spending less time in his litter box because he will be absorbing most of the nutrients he consumes. There will be

little hard to digest plant matter or other filler which would cause a higher volume of waste products.

One word of caution... if you decide to feed a whole prey diet be sure you are purchasing your fert's food from a reputable source. If the prey animal has an illness, there's a possibility that it can be passed to your fert when he consumes it.

Raw carnivore diet: This may be a little more palatable to the average pet owner than watching your fert consume a whole animal. There are some commercially prepared raw food diets on the market that come either frozen or freeze-dried. Check the label if you decide to feed one of these. You'll want to avoid some of the foods prepared for dogs because these may contain vegetables and other plant matter.

 There is some debate among those who choose to feed a natural diet on whether live or dead animals should be used. In most cases it comes down to personal choice — yours and your fuzzy's, and always in consultation with a veterinarian.

Treats

Dennis always shared a strong bond with Chester, his four-year-old, sable ferret. Chester was often with Dennis, including during dinner time or when Dennis was relaxing in front of the television with a snack. Dennis felt bad if he didn't share his food with Chester, so he often gave Chester vegetables from his plate or popcorn, fruit and cereal when he was snacking.

Chester was especially fond of ice cream. What had started as a treat every now and then turned into an everyday occurrence, and Dennis and Chester often unwound after a long day with a scoop of vanilla ice cream.

Over time, Dennis noticed some changes in Chester. First he attributed Chester's preference to lounge next to him rather than run and play the way he used to as a sign of aging. When Dennis noticed that Chester was putting on weight and not as interested in his regular food, however, he knew there was a problem. Add to that some smelly diarrhea, and Dennis knew it was time for a trip to Chester's veterinarian.

As it turned out, Chester was suffering the effects of a poor diet. His veterinarian put him on a restricted diet with only a few treats each day. And no ice cream! Dennis was heartbroken when he realized that he was literally killing Chester with what he had perceived as kindness. He was relieved that they had caught the problem early enough to avoid more serious complications for Chester's health. Chester was resistant to his new diet at first, but after several months he was back to his old mischievous self!

From Dennis and Chester's story we can learn a valuable lesson. When giving your ferret treats, moderation is key. With a proper diet and no more than one or two treats a day, you will have a happy and healthy fert on your hands.

Some favorite treats for ferrets include: raisins, banana slices, low-sugar cereals, cooked meats, vitamin supplements, melons, apples, hard-boiled eggs, and creamy peanut butter.

It cannot be stressed enough that these things be limited to one or two per day. Most treat have absolutely no nutritional value for your fert, and he will be unable to properly digest most of them. If you feed too many, you may find that your fuzzy's appetite for his regular food decreases and may lead to illness and obesity.

No-Nos

Although there are many foods that are fine when fed to your fert in small quantities, there are some foods that should be avoided altogether, such as non-organic fruit and vegetables. If you give your fuzzy fruits or vegetables as treats, select organic produce. The pesticides and other chemicals that are used to treat much of our produce can wreak havoc on your fuzzball's digestive system, and in some cases, may prove fatal.

Also, when feeding vegetables, they should always be cooked. Raw produce can cause intestinal blockages.

Some other foods to avoid include:

- ✔ Chocolate.

- ✔ Raw egg whites.

- ✔ Seeds and nuts.

- ✔ Sugar-laden foods.

Water

Just like us, your ferret needs to drink water every day. So be sure his water bottle is filled with fresh, clean water each day. To avoid your fuzzy ingesting harmful bacteria, make sure to clean the bowl too (a 1-minute chore most ferret owners neglect) using non-toxic, organic dish soap. Also, make sure the water bowl is not too big (don't use a water bucket in other words), because ferrets can drown.

The Nuts and Bolts of Feeding Your Fert

As we mentioned in Chapter 5, you must purchase a water bottle and food bowl suitable for your fert's needs. This mostly means ferret-proof bowls. To keep messes to a minimum, use these two foolproof fixes:

1. Find a bowl that is hard for your ferret to tip over.

2. Find a bowl that can be secured to your fuzzy's cage.

Your ferret still may enjoy flinging his food around, but doing these two fixes will keep him from really going wild.

You should also ensure that his water bottle is tightly secured to the cage. As intelligent and crafty as these little guys are, they have been known to reach through the bars of their cages to dislodge their water bottles.

 Keep food bowls out of corners. Remember, your fert likes to back into corners to use the bathroom. You can avoid having his food bowl contaminated this way ever again by keeping it elsewhere. If his food bowl does become soiled, be sure to remove it and wash it thoroughly as soon as possible to remove the scent that says, "This is a toilet."

Free feeding is usually the best way to feed your fert. This means that there will be food and water available to him at all times. A ferret's fast metabolism causes food to move quickly through his digestive system. This means he is ready for his next meal within three to four hours of eating his last one.

Usually it works out fine to leave food available for your ferret all the time. Most fuzzies will only eat as much as they need. Keep a close eye on your fert's weight, however. If he is gaining weight, he may need to be fed only enough for one meal every three to four hours.

He may also need to change to a different food. Not getting the proper nutrients from the food they're eating is one reason ferts may overeat. If you are concerned with your fert's weight or eating habits, see your veterinarian.

Giving Your Fert Dietary Supplements

There are several dietary supplements on the market geared toward ferrets, such as Linatone, Ferratone and Ferretive. The first two supplements can help keep your fert's coat and skin healthy, shiny and free of flakes. The second is a nutritional supplement used to increase your fuzzy's caloric intake. These supplements are available from your veterinarian or at pet supply stores.

Many people wonder if their ferret needs a dietary supplement. If you are feeding your fert a diet that adequately meets his nutritional needs, he will probably do fine without the supplement. Many ferts love the taste of them, however, so you may want to keep them on hand as treats. Again, use them as treats in moderation.

The high calorie supplements are usually only needed for ailing ferts. Unless you are using them in very small quantities as treats, you should only give these supplements to your ferret following the advice of your veterinarian. It's not a good idea to decide on how much and how often your sickly fuzzy needs the extra calories on your own.

Chapter 8: Taking Care of Ferret

Taking care of your fuzzy requires more than just housing, feeding and ferret-proofing. It's also important that you handle your ferret properly, and that you help him to enjoy and look forward to your attention. You'll also be spending time cleaning his cage and grooming him.

Plus there will be times when you travel or need to be away from home for extended periods of time. Do you leave your fur kid home or take him on the road? This chapter will help you with the day-to-day care of your fert.

Handling and Picking Up Your Fuzzy

Like most people who share their lives with ferrets, you are surely going to want to cuddle and hold your fuzzy. Even if you're not the cuddly type, there are also going to be times when it's necessary to pick up your ferret in order to groom him, medicate him or move him out of danger. It's important that you know the proper way to handle your fuzzball and work on developing a relationship with him so he comes to trust you and enjoy your attention.

Before you lift up your fert, you should:

- **Be sure he is awake and alert.** Waking a ferret from a sound sleep to cuddle is not a good way to make friends.

- **Ensure that he knows you're there.** Don't just swoop down and grab your fert. Startling him in this way can put him on the defensive and result in him biting you.

- **Have some treats on hand.** Giving a few small treats to your ferret while you are handling him is a great way to create a positive correlation in his mind. Your fur kid will quickly understand that, "Hey, every time mom picks me up, good things happen. I hope she'll want to cuddle again soon!"

- **Let him come to you.** Unless it is an absolute emergency, try to wait until your ferret seeks your attention. This is a great way to build his trust in you.

- **Use both hands** when you're ready to pick up your fert for some snuggle and play time. Gently lift him close to your body. You should always support his whole body, ensuring that all four of his feet are either in your hands or supported against your body.

 Don't expect your ferret to sit still in your arms. These inquisitive creatures are usually ready for some action. Once you've got them in your arms, it's likely they' ll try to climb over your chest, shoulders and anything else they can get their paws on.

Supervise children if you allow them to pick up your fuzzball. Children have a tendency to give tight hugs or squeeze too hard around the ferret's body. This can lead to the child being bitten as the fert tries to defend himself. Don't put your child or your ferret in this position.

Grooming Your Fert

Bathing

Plan on spending some time each month grooming your ferret. Grooming includes bathing, trimming nails and cleaning ears. Fortunately you can do all these things yourself at home, without too much effort (I promise!).

The idea of bathing your fuzzy may seem a bit daunting, but it can be done. A good place to do the bathing is in your kitchen sink. Here you'll be able to stand comfortably, keep a good grip on your fert, and control the flow and temperature of the water.

Bathing your fert involves a simple 8-step system:

1. Be sure that your fert has used the litter box before you give him a bath, otherwise he may quickly dirty the bath water.

2. There's nothing worse than getting your ferret into the bath and then realizing you've forgotten shampoo or towels. Be sure you have everything you'll need on hand before putting him in the tub.

3. Fill the sink with enough water to get your ferret good and wet, but still allows your fuzzy to have all four feet on the ground. This will help him

to feel secure while you give him a bath.

4. Choose a mild shampoo, such as a baby shampoo or a shampoo designed for cats and kittens. If you are uncertain about which shampoo will be best for your ferret, or if your ferret has dry skin or another skin condition, ask your veterinarian for shampoo.

5. Keep the temperature of the water warm, but not too hot.

6. Gently lather the ferret with the shampoo, taking special care to keep the soap out of his eyes, mouth and ears.

7. Empty the tub of the dirty water and begin to rinse your fert with warm, clean water. Be sure to remove all the shampoo from your ferret's fur.

8. Once your ferret is clean and rinsed, thoroughly dry him with a towel. Some ferts are tolerant of a hair dryer as long as you keep it on a low setting, keep it moving and keep it a foot or more away from the ferret's body.

 If you accidentally get soap in your ferret's eyes, rinse his face very gently with a small amount of water at a time until his eyes are clear.

Plan on bathing your ferret once a month or so. Bathing him more often than this can cause his odor to become even stronger, believe it or not. The musky scent we associate with ferrets is due to oils in their skin. If you give your fuzzball too many baths, he will begin to produce even more oils to make up for the oil that was washed away. This in turn will cause an even stronger odor than usual. Too many baths can also lead to dry skin and a dull, coarse coat.

Ear Cleaning

Once your fert is clean and fresh as a daisy, you can think about cleaning his ears and trimming his nails. Ear cleaning usually needs to be done once a month and is usually easy unless your fuzzy has ear mites or another condition that may cause build-up in his ears.

If you see an abnormal amount of build-up in your ferret's ears or if the build-up is black or there is an odor, you should see your veterinarian before cleaning his ears.

Other than those situations, you can clean your fert's ears with an over-the-counter ear cleanser which can be found at most pet supply stores. Put a few drops in each ear (make sure you are following the directions on the package) and allow your fuzzy to shake loose any build-up.

You can then proceed to wipe the outer part of the ear with a piece of cotton and you're finished.

If your fert is unhappy with having his ears wiped out, you may need to scruff him (i.e. hold the scruff of his neck) or have someone else scruff him while you finish cleaning.

Nail Trimming

Ear cleaning was a cinch. Trimming your fuzzy's nails, however, is a different story. Having their nails trimmed is not usually one of ferret's favorite pastimes.

Try making grooming time easier for both of you by offering him a treat. This has two benefits. First, he'll be distracted from what you are doing to his feet, and secondly, he'll make a positive association between getting a treat and having his nails trimmed.

Trimming your ferret's nails is usually easiest if you have someone helping you do it. One of you can scruff your fuzzy while the other does the trimming. You can use a regular toenail clipper that you would use on yourself or you can use a baby's nail clipper.

 There is a vein that runs through the fert's claws that can be seen through the nail. This vein is called the quick. It's very important that you choose a spot above the quick to trim. If you trim too far down and hit the quick, you can cause your ferret a great deal of pain and he will bleed quite a bit. Keep a styptic pencil handy in case you need to stop a nail from bleeding.

To clip your ferret's nails you should:

- Hold the paw you are working on firmly with your thumb pressing up from the bottom of the foot. This should enable you to trim each nail separately.

- Locate the quick in your fert's nail.

- Place the clippers on a spot slightly above the quick, and clip the nail in one fast clip.

- Continue trimming nails in this manner until they are all clipped.

 Nail trimming time is also a good time to inspect the pads of your fert's feet. Just like our feet, these sensitive pads can get dry, rough, and cracked. If you notice this is the case with your fuzzy's feet, you can apply a bit of petroleum jelly to soothe and smooth his foot pads.

Dental Care

The health of your fuzzy's teeth is vital to his overall health. A ferret with tooth decay and tooth loss will very often not be able to eat well, causing weight loss and other health problems (and eventually death). In addition, the runaway bacterial growth in your fert's mouth that comes with diseased gums can cause a whole host of other illnesses.

The best way to avoid the health problems caused by gum disease and tooth decay is to make a dental check-up part of your regular yearly visit to the veterinarian. If your vet detects tartar build-up or other problems, he can put your fert under a general anesthesia and clean your fuzzball's teeth or extract a tooth if necessary.

Some people attempt to brush and check their ferrets' teeth on their own. It's entirely up to you (and your fur kid) if you want to do this. Usually feeding your ferret a proper diet is the #1 way to keep your fert's teeth healthy -- and if you switch you little guy or girl to a pure, 100% natural raw-food diet, their teeth will be pristine.

Using a toothbrush designed especially for small pets or a strip of gauze rubbed gently along your ferret's teeth can help prevent tooth decay and gum disease. The process should be done very gently, and only if your comfort level allows. If you are unsure about how to do this, ask your vet to show you how to do it.

Cleaning Your Fuzzball's Cage

Keeping your ferret's cage clean and tidy is an important part of his care, as well as vital to odor control. A dirty cage is by far the main culprit for the foul odor people sometimes associate with ferrets.

Cleaning the cage involves cleaning the floor and bars of the cage, food bowls, water bottles, litter box, bedding (especially) and toys. Whoo! You can get tired just thinking about it, but it is important to your fert's health and well-being.

Three little but powerful actions you can do daily to create a sanitary home for your fert (which makes a tremendous difference over time) are:

1. Scoop the litter box. This will keep poop and urine odor at a minimum. Your fert is also more likely to use a clean box. If the litter box becomes too full your fert may choose a new spot to eliminate... and it probably won't be in a spot you would have chosen.

2. Wash out food dishes before refilling them.

3. Check for any ripped or overly soiled toys or bedding. Pull these out and clean them or replace them with clean toys and bedding.

Weekly odor-killing tricks include:

- Doing a thorough cleaning of food bowls. Use a solution warm water and bleach to clean food particles and feces from the food bowls. Be sure to rinse the bowls thoroughly before refilling them with food.

- Scrubbing the water bottle with soap and warm water with a bottle brush.

- Emptying and scrubing out the litter box. Use warm soapy water and a scrub brush to get the box clean. A solution of vinegar and water works well on getting out tough urine stains.

- Washing or replacing all bedding.

- Washing or replacing soiled or ripped toys.

Every other week you should plan on doing a detailed cleaning of the cage itself to keep your furball happy, healthy and sparkling. To do this you need to:

- Remove everything from the cage.

- Sweep out all of the debris from the bottom of the cage and shelves.

- If the weather allows, take the cage outdoors and hose it down and scrub every nook and cranny with hot water and soap.

- If you are unable to take the cage outside, use rags and a scrub brush to scrub every corner of the cage with hot, soapy water.

- Dry the cage and replace bedding, toys, food bowls and litter box.

Traveling and Your Fert

At one time or another during your ferret's lifetime you are probably going to need to be away from home for a few days. Whether you have a short business trip or a long vacation planned, provisions will have to be made for your fur kid. The big question then is, do you leave your ferret at home or take him with you?

Taking Your Ferret on the Road

Before even considering taking your fuzzy on a trip with you, there are 8 questions you need to ask yourself:

1. Are ferrets legal in the area to which you are traveling?

2. Is your fert up to date on rabies vaccinations?

3. Does he have a clean bill of health from your veterinarian?

4. Is your ferret young and healthy enough to survive a stressful travel experience?

5. Do you have a cage that is acceptable for your mode of travel (car, airplane, train, etc.) and does it allow adequate space for your fuzzball to eat, sleep, eliminate and play?

6. If you are traveling other than by car (like on a train, plane, etc), have you checked with the company's standards to make sure you are allowed to travel with your fert and that you have everything the company requires for travel (pet taxi, identification tags, health certificate, reservation, etc)?

7. Do you have a leash and harness for him which will allow him to have plenty of playtime outside of his cage?

8. When you arrive at your destination, will you have enough time to devote to your ferret's care and exercise needs?

If you answered *no* to any of these questions, you may want to rethink taking your furball along on vacation with you.

If, after considering all of these questions carefully, you still feel that your ferret would make a great traveling companion, there are a few shortcuts to make traveling with your fuzzy easier:

- Make sure your ferret has an adequate supply of food and water for the trip.

- Keep your fuzzy in his cage at all times while driving. Allowing him the run of the car can be dangerous.

- Plan on regular stops to allow your fert some time out of his cage (on leash and harness, of course) if you have a long trip planned.

- Carry copies of your fert's rabies and health certificates on hand at all times.

- Be sure to pack any medication that your ferret is currently taking.

- Never leave your fert alone in the car if the temperature is extreme. Animals can quickly succumb to heat stroke or hypothermia if left in the car.

- If you are flying or taking a mode of transportation other than your own vehicle, be sure that you meet all of the company's requirements for traveling with your pet.

- Put your contact information on your fert's cage.

- Make sure your fuzzy is welcome at the home, hotel or resort where you will be staying.

 You may need to take a little time to ferret-proof the place where you are staying. If this isn't possible, then plan on keeping your ferret on his leash and harness when he isn't in his cage. Nothing can ruin your good time faster than having your ferret do major damage to your hotel room, or worse, having him become ill or die because he got into something.

Leaving Home Without Him

There may be occasions when taking your fuzzball away with you is not an option. Or you may decide that you don't want to worry about scooping litter boxes and ferret-proofing hotel rooms while you are on vacation. Whatever the reason for leaving him behind, there are several options when you aren't planning on traveling with your fert.

Pet sitters. This is one of the best options. Having a petsitter come to your home to take care of your ferret means your fuzzy gets to stay in the comfort of his own home and stick to his routine while you are away.

You'll want to check references before hiring anyone. Remember, this person needs to be reliable enough to entrust your pets and your home with while you are out of town. Plan on having your petsitter spend a little time with you and your pets before you leave so she can get to know your ferret's routines and habits.

Pet hotels and boarding facilities. You may choose to board your ferret at a pet hotel or with your veterinarian. Check out any facility thoroughly before leaving your pet there. There are many reputable boarding facilities out there, but there are also many who do nothing more than warehouse your pet while you're away.

Boarding facilities may require you to provide your pets' health records. Be sure to ask how much playtime your fuzzy will get outside of his cage each day. Many places will not provide a cage as spacious as the one you have at home so this is especially important.

In some cases, boarding facilities do no more than board and feed your pet for you -- meaning they aren't going to provide extra playtime and socialization. You also run the risk of your pet picking up an illness from other animals at these facilities.

Whether you decide to use a pet sitter or a boarding facility you will need to leave some information for them. You should leave:

- All your contact information, including the name, address and phone number of the place you will be staying.

- An emergency contact, such as a friend, family member or neighbor in case you can't be reached immediately.

- Explicit, written instructions on the care and feeding of your fuzzy, including specific information on food, treats, and medications.

- Your veterinarian's contact information.

No matter which option you choose when leaving your pet, you may want to consider contacting your vet before you go. Let them know that you will be leaving your pet in someone's care. You can tell your vet that this person or facility has your permission to make medical decisions for your ferret in your absence, and talk about payment arrangements.

Chapter 9: It's Playtime!

Despite the fact that it sometimes seems your fuzzy's greatest joy in life is napping, you better believe he takes his playtime seriously!

As any animal behaviorist or zookeeper will tell you, mental stimulation is a vital component of any animal's health and well being. Left in his cage without daily exercise that involves playing with his favorite human companion can cause your fert to become depressed and anxious. This condition is commonly referred to as being *cage crazy*.

Let's try to picture what can happen to your ferret without the benefits and added stimulation of playtime and exercise outside of the cage. Imagine yourself sitting in a stuffy room listening to a lecture on a topic that you find mind-numbingly boring. The lecturer is speaking in a monotone and droning on and on. Can you see yourself sitting there, shifting around on the uncomfortable chair?

Now imagine that you have to sit there day in and day out for the rest of your life. What would you do? How long would it take before you went completely out of your mind? This is what it would be like for your ferret to be stuck in his cage forever with nothing extra added to enrich his life.

So, now that you understand the importance of providing stimulation for your fuzzball, let's look at the best toys, enrichment activities and games to play with your ferret.

Toys

There are a lot of possibilities out there when it comes to toys for your fert. Check out your local pet supply store and you'll find tons to choose from.

You won't want to limit your toy choices to those you can find in a store, however. There are plenty of things you can find around your house that will amuse your fert at no cost.

 When you're looking for toys for your fuzzy, don't overlook the cat aisles. Ferrets can be entertained for hours by cat toys.

Some ferret favorites include:

- **Long wands with feathers at the end.** These can be dangled over your fert's head or dragged around a room so he can chase them.

"Pass it to me!"
Photo by Dawn Landrum, Landrum Arts
http://LandrumArtsLA.com

- **Balls.** Your ferret can run himself ragged running after and rolling balls. For even more fun, you can get him one of the balls with bells or that makes squeaky noises as he pushes them around.

- **Squeaky toys.** These are a great way to get your fert's attention and get him to come running.

- **Stuffed animals.** Your fuzzy can rough-house and roll around with these.

- **Tunnels.** You can create complicated mazes for your ferret to work his way through. You can buy these at pet stores or make your own out of cardboard rolls.

- **Dig boxes.** If your ferret is like most, he'll love to dig. The problem has always been, what do you let them dig in that is safe for them? One company is now selling cardboard boxes full of packaging materials (peanuts) made of starch. It's completely bio-degradable so even if your fert swallows some, you know it will break down rather than causing blockages. You can find this product at a discount at http://findoutaboutferrets.com/digbox

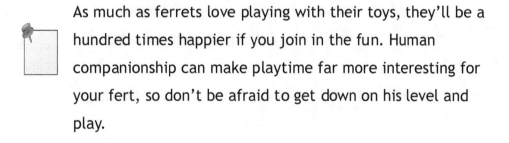

Make it a regular practice to check on your ferret's toys. Remove any toys that have been damaged. Stuffed animals that are torn or plastic toys that your ferret has chewed on can be ingested and cause blockages in your fert.

As much as ferrets love playing with their toys, they'll be a hundred times happier if you join in the fun. Human companionship can make playtime far more interesting for your fert, so don't be afraid to get down on his level and play.

Positive Reinforcement Training

There's nothing better to get the wheels turning in your ferret's head than teaching him a few tricks. Training can be fun for both you and your fuzzy if you follow these 7 silent techniques that magnetically make your ferret want to obey your every command:

1. Keep training sessions short. Your ferret can get bored or frustrated pretty quickly so try to keep training sessions to about ten minutes.

2. Always use treats to reward your fert once he performs the trick you want. Think of it as giving him a paycheck for a job well done. Treats are the key to keeping him motivated.

3. Keep the treats small so he isn't overindulging on things that aren't giving him much nutrition.

4. Be patient. Teaching your fert new tricks may take a little time, but the point of it is to have fun.

5. Give your ferret a little running around time outside of his cage before trying to get his attention for training.

6. Use the treats as a lure. Show your ferret the treat and then move it in front of his nose so he can follow it into whatever position you are hoping to achieve (standing up, rolling over, etc.).

7. You may need to teach complicated tricks in stages.

Let's take a look at the step-by-step process of teaching your fuzzy some tricks:

Beg

Getting your fert to stand on his hind legs to "beg" for a treat is fairly easy to train. Take a small treat and hold it in front of your fuzzy's nose. Give him the command, "Beg." Slowly move the treat up over your ferret's head. His head will follow the treat, and he will raise himself up onto his hind legs when the treat is raised just out of his reach.

As soon as he is in this position, tell him, "Good (or any other word you choose to mark the correct behavior)." Let him have the treat at the same time.

Repeat this sequence over several short training sessions. You will soon have a fert who is sitting up and begging for his treats all the time.

Roll over

This trick is a littler tougher and may need to be taught in a few stages.

Wait until your fert is lying down. Hold a treat near his nose and slowly move it to the side. Once he starts turning his head toward the treat, begin moving the treat around toward the back of your ferret's head.

If you find that you're getting your ferret to move his head, and then losing him when you bring the treat around his head, start giving him the treat for turning his head. Once he's gotten this down, raise your expectations -- he only gets his treat if he turns his head past a certain spot.

Continue building on the head turn until you can move the treat all the way around his head, at this point your ferret will need to roll his entire body over in order to get the treat. Voila, you ferret is rolling over!

To raise the difficulty, add the command, "Roll over." Say this when you first show him the treat, and then do as you've been doing, moving the treat around his head until he rolls over. With a great deal of practice, you may be able to get your ferret to roll over on command without using the treat as a lure. (Don't be disappointed if you never get to this point. This is a tough trick, and remember, the point is to get your ferret thinking, not to get you frustrated.)

Come here

This trick is useful not just for impressing your friends but also in case your fuzzy runs outside and escapes. Like anything else, coming when called is a simple matter of positive reinforcement training. Just have a phrase like "come here" that you say consistently when you want this trick done. When your fert comes to you, give him a treat. Eventually, your little guy will link the sound "come here" with running to you and getting a reward.

 Using the positive reinforcement method of training, you can teach your ferret a multitude of tricks. Get as creative as you want (for instance, one person I know has trained her fuzzy to "play dead" by rolling over on his back). Just remember to have fun!

 A great book to learn more about positive reinforcement training is _Don't Shoot the Dog: The New Art of Teaching and Training_ by Karen Pryor. This book will give you the basics of training any type of animal. Learn more at http://findoutaboutferrets.com/pryor

Enriching Your Fert's Life

As intelligent and inquisitive as ferrets are, they are happiest when we keep their environment interesting. This isn't hard to do, and the longer you share your life with a fuzzy, the more ideas you'll come up with. Here are a few to get you started:

- Don't bring the same toys out for every playtime. Changing the toys will keep things interesting.

- Remove the toys from your ferret's cage and put different ones in every few days. Switching them around will add some extra stimulation to your fert's day even when you aren't there to play with him.

- Play hide and seek with a portion of his food. You can hide food or a few small treats around his cage or around the room he is playing in.

- Take him to a new spot to explore next time you take him out for a walk.

- Let him explore a new (ferret-proofed) room that he's never been allowed in before.

 It's vital to remember that exercise and playtime are a big issue for your ferret. It was said earlier in this book, but it bears repeating, that ferrets are not like hamsters, mice or guinea pigs that can live happily ever after in their cage. A ferret will never be happy this way. Leaving your ferret locked in his cage for days on end with nothing new and interesting to engage him is pure torture for him and can cause some serious problems. Be sure you have the time to engage with your fuzzy before taking the big step of bringing one home.

Chapter 10: Elbows Off the Table

In this chapter we'll take a look at ferret behavior and common behavioral problems. We'll talk about how to avoid or eliminate unwanted behaviors such as nipping and house soiling.

Fert Behavior

Although all fuzzies have their own personalities, there are some behaviors that are common to all of them to one extent or another. Let's take a look at some of these behaviors:

Body Language

The best way to tell what your ferret is thinking is to watch what he's doing with his body. Three non-verbal clues to look for include:

- Flinging their bodies in every direction, sidestepping in a prancing movement, and twisting around quickly. Ferts usually do this "happy dance" when they are feeling frisky and playful. It's all a part of having a good time.

- A puffed up tail. This silent signal indicates that your fert is upset or excited.

- An arched back accompanied by an open mouth and a shrieking sound should tell anyone approaching to back off. A ferret displaying this type of body language is not a happy camper, and may even be about to show some aggression. It may be spurred by anger, fear or pain. It may also be accompanied by a spray of musk if your fert hasn't been descented yet.

Vocalization

Although your fuzzy is quiet most of the time, he does on occasion feel the need to do some talking. The strange sounds coming from your fert may concern you at first, but take heart -- most of it is very normal fuzzy behavior.

Wonder what your ferret is trying to tell you? Here are a few ways in which ferts vocalize:

- **Dooking.** This is the most common form of ferret-speak. At first you may feel a bit paranoid that someone is laughing behind your back. Never fear... that chuckling sound you hear is your ferret, and when he's making that noise it means he's having a grand old time. The more excited he gets, the more dooking he'll do.

- **Barking.** This is a short sound of disapproval that your ferret may make from time to time. He usually makes it to show that he's unhappy with something, like someone else playing with his favorite toy or stealing his food.

- **Shrieking and hissing.** If you hear your fert making a high pitch screeching sound accompanied by some fast-paced chatter or if you hear some hissing, watch out. These sounds mean that your ferret is annoyed, disturbed or afraid. When a ferret makes these sounds, he is more likely to act in an aggressive manner if cornered or put in a situation he finds uncomfortable.

Socializing

If you share your life with more than one fur kid, or if you schedule play dates with other ferts, you may see some things that you find disconcerting. Usually, however, the behaviors that you feel may be a cause for concern are really just typical ferret play. Some common things that occur when ferrets play are:

- **Roughhousing.** Ferrets seem to love a rough and tumble kind of play. It's not uncommon for them to wrestle or nip one another.

- **Alpha rolling.** This involves one fuzzy grabbing another by the scruff of his neck and flipping him over onto his back. In this manner, one ferret may be establishing his dominance over another.

 If your ferrets' play seems to be getting out of hand, if one of them appears frightened or is continuously shrieking, or if one of them draws blood, end the play immediately. This is probably more than just roughhousing.

Some Other Fuzzy Behavior

In addition to their amusing antics, scintillating conversation and shaky social skills, ferrets have a few other tricks up their proverbial sleeves when it comes to behavior. These include:

- **Hoarding.** Ferrets love to find new treasures, and pretty much anything falls into this category. They're famous for finding and hiding all manner of objects. It's also not uncommon for them to become obsessed with a particular object. A fert with an object obsession will carry it around, and if someone tries to take it away from him, he'll get very stressed.

- **Prey behaviors.** As cute as they are, it's sometimes tough to remember that fuzzies are natural predators. Despite the fact that their meals are now being served up to them, there are some instinctive behaviors that can come out while they're playing that mimic the act of hunting and chasing food. Roll a ball in front of your fert, and you watch him chase it down. You may also catch your ferret sitting still for a moment (yes, it does occasionally happen!) waiting and watching only to pounce on the feet of some unsuspecting human.

- **Digging.** Since their closest wild relatives are burrowers, it's not hard to understand why your fuzzy exhibits this behavior.

 If you find that your fert is digging more than seems normal, there may be something other than a burrowing instinct at work. Make sure that you are giving your ferret plenty of exercise and stimulation (see Chapter 9). Digging can be a sign that your fuzzy is going a little stir crazy from being cooped up in his cage too much.

Training Your Fuzzy

Many of the ferrets who end up in shelters are brought there because of behavior problems, such as nipping or not using the litter box. The saddest part about this is that in most cases if their owners had invested a little more time training their fert, they would have ended up sharing their life with a well-behaved pet.

 Start training your ferret from the day you bring him home. It is much easier to establish good behaviors than it is to eliminate bad ones.

One of the best methods of training any species is positive reinforcement training. We discussed this a little bit in Chapter 9. Basically, this training method involves pairing a desired behavior with a reward (think Pavlov's dog).

An example of this would be giving your ferret a treat when he uses his litter box. If this happens several times your fert begins to realize that he gets a goody every time he eliminates in his litter box, but nothing happens when he eliminates elsewhere. He'll quickly learn it's worth the effort to eliminate in his litter box.

 The best part of positive reinforcement training is that it helps you to build a trusting bond with your fert. Your fuzzy quickly learns that when you're around good things happen for him.

Let's take a closer look at how to use this method to train you ferret.

Litter Training

The most important thing to remember when you set out to train your ferret to use his litter box is patience. Some fuzzies catch on quickly while others take a little longer to get it. There are 5 confidential shortcuts you can use to help speed him along...

1. Keep your ferret confined to his cage until he has mastered the art of using the litter box.

2. If you have a large cage for your fuzzy, confine him to just a portion of it until he gets the hang of using his litter box. Even when he starts to get it, once he strays too far from the box, any corner will do when he has to go.

3. Let your fert chose his own potty area, and then put the litter box there. Ferrets are clean animals who usually choose one spot which they'll use to eliminate in. It's much easier to allow your ferret to choose his spot and then place his box there than it is to try to force your fuzzy to use the corner you designate as the bathroom.

4. Give your ferret lots of praise and a small treat when he uses his litter box.

5. Once your ferret has mastered the art of litter box use, you can allow him the full run of his cage and playtime outside of the cage. You should have a litter box handy for him to use while he is out and about.

Remember, ferrets have very short digestive systems which means they'll need to eliminate frequently. Again, allow your fert to choose his spot, and then place the litter box there.

 Expect mistakes. Even the most well-trained ferret can have the occasional accident. Keep a product like Nature's Miracle on hand to clean up any accidents. This type of cleaning product is designed specifically to clean up urine and feces and take the odor out. It (or something similar) can be found in most pet supply stores.

If your fuzzy has been using his litter box consistently for awhile and then suddenly stops, here's what to do:

- Have your veterinarian examine your fert to make sure there is no underlying health issue making it difficult to get to the litter box in time.

- Make sure you're cleaning his litter box frequently. A dirty litter box will cause your ferret to find a new place to use the bathroom.

- If your fuzzy has had any upheavals in his otherwise peaceful existence (moving, getting a new ferret, change in schedule, etc) it's not uncommon for his stress to manifest itself by having accidents outside of the litter box. If you believe this is the case, start back at square one with his litter training and give him a little time to get used to the new situation.

Dealing with Nipping and Biting

There is a difference between nipping and biting. Nipping is something that's often done as part of playing. Also, the younger the kit, the more likely he is to be nippy. Just like babies of other species, ferrets have teething pain. It feels good to them to bite, but it's important they learn as early as possible that it's never okay for them to use their teeth on someone's skin.

To help you teach your fuzzy not to nip, I have developed a breakthrough anti-nip technology called TED, which stands for:

*T*oys to chew on

*E*nd something good

*D*eter nipping your skin

TED is so simple and fun, even your child could do it. Here's how TED works, so that you never need to worry about your ferret biting you again:

Toys. Provide lots of toys for your ferret to chew on. If he begins to nip you while playing, you can tell him "no" and redirect him to a toy.

End something good. If your fuzzy refuses to be redirected toward a toy, you may need to try another tactic. The same way you teach your fert that when he does something good (using his litter box, performing a trick) he gets a treat, you should teach him that when he performs an undesirable behavior something good comes to an end.

For example, if your fert is out of his cage for playtime and decides that he is going to nip your hands as part of his good time, return him immediately to his cage. It won't take long for your intelligent fuzzy to learn that using his teeth on your skin puts a quick end to playtime.

Deter nipping your skin. Use a deterrent, such as pepper or Bitter Apple spray, on any of your exposed skin. Bitter Apple is something that can be purchased at most pet supply stores. One taste of one of these substances, and it's unlikely that your ferret will be rushing back for seconds.

 Begin nip training as soon as you possibly can. The process usually goes more smoothly with young kits than it does with older ferts who may never have had training. Nipping has had a longer time to become an established behavior for adults, so it's likely it will take a bit more training and patience before they understand that nipping is not okay.

Biting is a different matter. Biting is an aggressive reaction to fear, pain, or stress. A bite usually hurts more than a playful nip, and may even break the skin.

But the good news is that ferrets don't bite as often people seem to think they do. You're in far more danger of being bitten by a cat, dog, or another person than you are a ferret... but it does occasionally happen.

Bite prevention is the best way you can handle fert aggression. Some guaranteed methods proven to work include:

- Make sure your fuzzy knows you're there before you pick him up. Call his name or make some noise as you approach him. If you just swoop in and snatch up your ferret, you may startle him into a bite.

- Don't let your ferret get caught in uncomfortable situations. If a child is chasing him or someone has him cornered, remove him from the situation before he feels the need to defend himself.

- Don't let your fert have the upper hand. If he puts his teeth against your skin to try and coerce you into putting him down, tell him "no" or "wrong" and continue holding him for a few more minutes before returning him to his cage. It's important that you teach him that his bad behavior is not a good way to get what he wants.

- Make transitions as easy as possible for your fuzzy. Bringing home a new baby, another fert or moving are all things that can cause your ferret to become stressed out. Make a point of sticking to his usual schedule and giving him some extra attention in these situations.

- Bring him to the vet for regular check-ups. Aggression can be triggered by an underlying health issue. If your ferret shows signs of aggression seemingly out of the blue, your first step should be a trip to the vet.

Ferrets who have lived in abusive situations often spend a great deal of time feeling stressed and fearful, and are used to being put into a position to defend themselves. These fuzzies are probably not the best bet for a new ferret owner. If you are adopting an adult, be sure to ask about his history before you bring him home.

 Never, never, never use aggressive measures to punish your ferret for biting. Aggression breeds aggression. This will just put your fert in a position where he is constantly feeling fearful, and will be more likely to strike out.

Other Unwanted Behaviors

All ferrets are unique, so chances are your fuzzy will have some behaviors all his own that drive you absolutely nuts. Some ferts are big chewers and will gnaw on anything from your hand to the kitchen table. Others love to dig, and they don't care where they do it, and will make a beeline for the cat's litter box or a rare potted plant any chance they get.

Whatever undesirable behavior your ferret is performing, you can use the same techniques to eliminate them as you use for litter and nip training. A few practical solutions to keep in mind:

- Don't simply try to eliminate behaviors; replace unwanted behaviors with something else. For example, if you have a fert who loves to chew, don't just stop him from chewing on your table leg and expect him to never try it again.

- Chewing obviously fulfills some need for him so when you teach him not to chew the table, redirect him to a toy that is okay for him to chew.

- Undesirable behaviors should cause a loss of privileges. For example, a ferret who decides to go to the bathroom all over your living room should not be allowed to run around in that room until he has a better handle on using his litter box.

- Reward good behaviors. This should be done when you are actively training *and* when your ferret demonstrates good behavior during the normal course of his day. You'll find ample opportunities to reward your ferret without even trying.

- Prevention is key. If your fuzzy likes to dig, don't leave houseplants within his reach. If your ferret has a tendency to nip when he's cornered, don't allow anyone to corner him.

- Physical punishment is never an acceptable method of training your ferret.

 Keep in mind that many of your fert's annoying habits are perfectly normal ferret behaviors. Digging and chewing are instinctive behaviors which means your best bet in keeping your fuzzy from doing them in places you wish they wouldn't is to provide an acceptable outlet for them to do them in. Provide chew toys for the chewer or a digging box for your digger. This way you'll both be happy.

 Often when your ferret is digging, chewing, nipping or performing any other unwanted behavior to excess, it's a sign of boredom. Bring in some new toys, give him some more attention and more playtime outside of his cage and you may find these behaviors go away on their own. In Chapter 9, you'll find more ideas on providing a stimulating environment for your fuzzy.

Chapter 11: Let's Get Physical

Once you bring your ferret home, he's going to need regular veterinary care, including vaccinations, physicals, and treatment for illnesses. In this chapter we'll discuss the routine health care your ferret requires for a long, happy life.

Finding a Veterinarian

Not all veterinarians are created equal... at least not when it comes to caring for your fert. Many vets see dogs and cats all day with the occasional ferret thrown in. They may not be the best choice for your fuzzy. It's important that you find a veterinarian who is an expert in ferret care.

You should begin your search before you bring your fert home. A good place to start is to ask the breeder or shelter staff where you get your ferret to recommend a veterinarian. There are a few things you should look for when you are making the decision. The veterinarian you choose should:

- Keep abreast of new developments in veterinary medicine related to ferrets.

- Regularly see ferrets in his/her practice.

- Have taken courses in addition to the regular veterinary medicine curriculum relating to ferret health.

- Have a contact for you to use in case your fuzzy needs emergency care after hours.

 Plan on bringing your fuzzy to see your veterinarian shortly after you bring him home. This will allow you to get a full health exam, as well any vaccinations, taken care of immediately. Plus it will give you a chance to see your vet in action.

Spaying and Neutering

If your ferret has not been altered prior to bringing him home, plan on having this done as soon as possible. Neutering male ferts can prevent aggression issues and keep him from marking. It also helps keep odors down to a minimum.

Plus, a male in rut is just not much fun to have around. With only one thing on his mind, he won't be too interested in socializing with you.

Spaying your female is vital to her health and well-being. Since female fuzzies stay in heat until they're bred, you can be endangering her health by leaving her unaltered unless you plan on mating her. If left in heat for too long, she runs the risk of developing a condition known as aplastic anemia. This condition can be fatal if not treated.

The only reason not to spay or neuter your ferts is if you plan on breeding them. Breeding is not something that should be done by someone brand new to ferret ownership. For more information on breeding your ferts see Chapter 13.

 Spay and neuter surgeries are fairly simple procedures, but there is some risk involved as your fuzzy will be put under anesthesia. This is one of several reasons it's important that you find a veterinarian who is experienced in ferret care.

If you get your ferret from a breeder, don't be surprised if there's a clause in the contract they have you sign requiring that you wait until your fert gets close to sexual maturity (no earlier than 6 months of age) before spaying or neutering.

They are doing this for good reason. A strong correlation has been found between ferrets who have been altered at an early age and high incidences of adrenal disease.

Vaccinations

To keep your fuzzy healthy, you should keep him up-to-date on rabies and distemper vaccines. Ferrets should get their first distemper shots as young kits. These vaccinations are usually given for the first time at eight weeks of age, again at twelve weeks, and once more at sixteen weeks of age.

If your fert is over twelve weeks of age when you bring him home, and you have no record of his previous vaccinations, he should receive a distemper shot on his first trip to the vet. About four weeks after this he should receive a second booster.

Different veterinarians may have slightly different vaccination schedules that they use for ferrets. As long as your ferret gets a series of three shots as a kit, or one shot and a follow-up a few weeks later as an adult, follow your vet's guidelines for vaccinations.

Rabies vaccinations are a must for all ferrets, and may even be required by law depending on the area you live. Unlike distemper shots, a series of shots are not needed to inoculate against rabies. Your ferret should receive his first rabies shot at around four months of age. The first vaccination is good for a year. After that, many of the rabies vaccines are good for up to three years.

 Ask your veterinarian about your state's rabies vaccination requirement. Although a rabies vaccination may be good for three years, state law may require you to vaccinate yearly or every other year.

One concern that comes up when having your fuzzy vaccinated is allergic reactions. Talk to your veterinarian about giving your ferret a dose of benedryl, or another antihistamine, prior to being vaccinated. Most likely the antihistamine will do no harm even if it isn't necessary, and if your ferret is allergic you'll be happy that you took this precaution.

 Keep a close watch over your fuzzy for a day or so following his vaccinations. If he is going to have a reaction to the shots, this is when it would occur. If you have any concerns about your ferret's health, if he is vomiting or has diarrhea, call your veterinarian immediately.

Fleas, Ear Mites and Other Parasites... Oh My!

In addition to vaccinations, your ferret's first trip to the vet should include a thorough examination for fleas, ticks, ear mites, intestinal parasites and heartworms. Left untreated these things can cause a variety of problems for your pet ranging from severe discomfort to death.

Fleas and Ticks

If your ferret has fleas, you can detect them by doing a close examination of his skin and fur. You may see the fleas moving on your ferret's body, or you may see flea dirt, the waste products that fleas leave behind, around your fert's scruff or on his belly. If a tick has taken up residence on your ferret, you will be able to see it when you examine his skin, as well. Be sure to check your fuzzy all over, including in his ears. Ticks will attach themselves to your fuzzy's skin. You'll see a brown bulging thing sticking out which will grow in size as the tick feeds.

If your ferret has fleas, you should:

- Bathe him thoroughly. Check with your veterinarian to find out which shampoo is best to use and safe for your pet.

- Comb all of the dead fleas and flea waste from your fert's fur.

- Remove all of the bedding and toys from his cage. Your best bet is to get rid of them and replace with fresh bedding.

- Give his cage a good scrubbing.

Once fleas have taken up residence in your home, they are tough to get rid of. If you suspect that the flea infestation has spread to your home, call your vet to discuss your options. You may need to use a flea bomb. As a last resort, call an exterminator.

To remove ticks, you should:

- Pour a small amount of rubbing alcohol over the tick. This will cause him to release his grip on your fert's skin.

- Use tweezers to pull it gently from your ferret's skin. Pull the tick straight out so you don't leave any parts of it behind.

There are several products on the market that will help prevent your fuzzy from being infected by fleas and ticks. The ones you see most commonly are Frontline and Advantage. These are topical liquids that are applied once a month between your fert's shoulder blades. Check the packaging of whichever treatment you decide to use to make sure that it is effective on both fleas and ticks.

Heartworm Disease

Animals acquire heartworms through the bite of an infected mosquito. The heartworm takes up residence in your fuzzy's heart and can cause a range of problems if left untreated, including death.

A simple blood test may tell you if your ferret is positive for heartworm. If the test is positive, your veterinarian can prescribe a course of treatment. If the test is negative, you can start your ferret on a monthly heartworm preventative, such as Heartguard.

Ear Mites

If your ferret seems to be digging into his ears a lot, and you're finding more than the usual amount of build-up in there, chances are he has ear mites. The black gunk in his ears is the waste products of these annoying parasites. Your veterinarian can confirm the diagnosis of ear mites by looking at some of the build-up under a microscope.

Treatment usually involves giving your fert's ears a thorough cleaning, and then applying an ointment twice daily for up to two weeks. This should be done under your vet's direction.

Other Internal Parasites

Not anyone's favorite subject, but one that must be addressed for the sake of your fuzzy's health. In addition to heartworm, ferrets are susceptible to a wide variety of intestinal and other internal parasites including tapeworms, hookworms, and roundworms.

Some symptoms you may notice if your fuzzy has parasites are weight loss, increase in appetite, loose stool or diarrhea, and bloody stool.

 Bring a stool sample with you when you visit your veterinarian. She can check to see if your fuzzy is infected with parasites, and prescribe the best treatment if necessary.

When to Take Your Fert to the Vet

Sometimes it's difficult to make a decision about whether or not your ferret's symptoms require the care of a veterinarian. When in doubt, err on the side of caution. Fuzzies are notoriously stoic when they are not feeling well, so by the time you suspect there is a problem he may be feeling pretty poor.

There are a few things to keep an eye out for. If your fert exhibits any of the following symptoms, you should seek medical attention as soon as possible.

- ✔ Unusually lethargic or listless
- ✔ Inability to urinate or defecate
- ✔ Loss of consciousness
- ✔ Seizures
- ✔ Bleeding wound
- ✔ Loss of appetite
- ✔ Labored breathing
- ✔ Excessive vomiting
- ✔ Excessive diarrhea

 Remember, you know your fuzzy better than anyone. If he exhibits any behavior that strikes you as odd and causes you concern, call the vet. It's better to overreact than not to react at all when it comes to your fur kid's health.

 One common error made by people new to sharing their lives with a fuzzy is mistaking shivering as a symptom of a serious illness. Shivering is one way in which your fert regulates his body temperature, so if he is shivering it is most likely not a problem. Of course, if he continues to shiver for awhile or if the shivering is accompanied by other symptoms, consult your veterinarian.

Be sure to keep emergency numbers (veterinarian, emergency veterinary clinic and poison control) in a place you can easily find them.

Caring for the Sick Ferret

One of the biggest concerns when your fuzzy is feeling under the weather is feeding him. Since ferrets have such a fast metabolism, they need to eat every few hours, and missing a few meals can cause some serious problems. If your ferret is unable to eat well on his own, it will be up to you to ensure that he is getting adequate nutrition. This isn't as difficult as it may sound.

The best way to get calories into your fert is to feed him what ferret owners refer to as "duck soup." To make this meal, puree your fert's regular food. You can then mix it with water and a calorie supplement such as Nutra-Cal or kitten milk replacement formula. You may also want to add a little baby food in a meat variety for taste.

The consistency of your duck soup should be like that of a cream soup. It can be a little thicker if your fert is able to eat a bit on his own or lick some off a spoon you're holding. You may need to make it a bit thinner if your fuzzy needs a little more encouragement to eat. In this case you'll need to feed him using an eye dropper or syringe.

Your ferret should be fed about four ounces of this soup mixture every four hours or so until he is able to eat on his own again. Remember, for a ferret who needs to be fed with a dropper or syringe, you need to feed him slowly, giving him enough time to swallow food at his own pace. Feeding him too much, too quickly, can cause him to choke or vomit.

Other than feeding your ferret, it's important that you follow the instructions of your veterinarian carefully when your fert is ill. Keep a close eye on him to make sure that he is improving. If at any time you feel that his condition is worsening, or if he does not appear to be improving, call your veterinarian.

Emergency Plan

Don't let your beloved fuzzy get lost in the shuffle if an emergency occurs that requires you to leave your home on short notice. It's a good idea to keep a few things close at hand in case of emergency. Your fuzzy's emergency kit should include:

- A carrier set up with some soft bedding and a litter box.

- Enough food to last him for several days.

- Enough water to last him for several days.

- Extra litter.

- Any medication he is currently taking.

If you need to leave your home on a moment's notice because of weather conditions -- fire, flood or other problems -- it will only take a minute to load up your fuzzy and the items he'll need for a few days away from home.

Some people put stickers on the windows or doors of their home to alert emergency service personnel that they have pets inside. It's a good idea in case an emergency occurs while you are away from home and unable to let an emergency crew know that you have animals in need of help inside.

Chapter 12: Common Health Problems

The good news is that ferrets are generally healthy critters. It's important, however, that you're aware of the most common health issues faced by your fert. Knowing what to look for and what you can do to prevent these ailments can mean the difference between life and death for your fuzzy.

Cold and Flu

Ferrets are extremely susceptible to many of the same cold and flu germs that humans are, plus some more that we are not. What this means during cold and flu season is that you must take some extra precautions with your fert. These illnesses can be passed through the air or from contact with an infected human or animal.

The best way to handle this illness is to prevent it. If you're suffering from a cold, have someone else care for your fuzzy for a few days. If this isn't an option, make sure you wash your hands thoroughly before handling your ferret.

Despite our best efforts, ferrets may still come down with a cold. Their symptoms are basically the same ones which afflict us when we have a cold, including:

- ✔ Discharge from the eyes and nose
- ✔ Loss of energy
- ✔ Loss of appetite
- ✔ Coughing
- ✔ Congestion
- ✔ Loose stool
- ✔ Fever

As with us, usually time, rest and extra fluids are what get your ferret over his cold. They do occasionally require more intensive medical treatment such as IV fluids or antibiotics. If your ferret's symptoms don't begin to improve after a few days, make an appointment with his veterinarian.

Canine Distemper

This is the disease which you are vaccinating your fert against from an early age. It is highly contagious, and can be passed from one animal to another or carried on clothing. This disease causes your fuzzy a tremendous amount of suffering, and it is also almost one hundred percent fatal.

For this reason, the kindest course of action is for the ferret to be put to sleep as soon as he is diagnosed.

Pets who are vaccinated have nothing to fear. If your fert hasn't had his inoculations, however, there are some symptoms that will tip you off to the fact that you're dealing with distemper, including loss of appetite, diarrhea, rash, vomiting, and seizures.

Keeping your ferret up-to-date on his vaccinations is vital to keep him healthy. Failing to have him vaccinated can cause him tremendous pain and ultimately death.

Intestinal Blockages

Intestinal blockages are fairly common problems for ferrets. These inquisitive creatures have a bad habit of picking up anything and everything and putting it in their mouths. Ferts are also blocked by hairballs on occasion.

If you suspect that your fuzzy has ingested something he shouldn't have, you should watch for these symptoms:

- ✔ Lack of a bowel movement, or very small bowel movement
- ✔ Vomiting
- ✔ Bloated, painful stomach
- ✔ Inability to eat
- ✔ Listlessness
- ✔ Weight loss

If your fert is exhibiting any of these symptoms, call your vet. A small obstruction may be treated with Laxatone, but a more serious problem may require surgery. Let your vet make the call, as intestinal blockages are serious problems that can lead to death if not properly treated.

Cancer

Ferts are prone to get several different types of cancers. Some of the more common are:

- **Adrenal disease.** This disease causes the adrenal glands to become enlarged and to secrete excessive amounts of hormones into the blood. Tumors or lesions may form on the glands. Among other things, adrenal disease causes baldness or patchy hair loss, aggression, anemia, and loss of appetite. Treatment usually means removing the adrenal gland that has been affected. A correlation has been noted between early age spay and neuter and adrenal disease. For this reason, you may be better off waiting until around six months of age to have your fuzzy altered.

- **Insulinoma.** This type of cancer attacks the pancreas, the organ responsible for regulating blood sugar. Tumors cause an overproduction of insulin which results in a rapid decrease in blood sugar. This condition causes your fert to become lethargic and weak, and you may notice him vomiting, displaying uncoordinated movements, losing weight and succumbing to tremors. This condition is not usually cured, but may be managed to some degree with surgery, drugs and diet. Your veterinarian can help you choose the best course of action to help prolong the life of your fuzzy for at least a few months. There is some evidence that a raw food diet, or natural diet, can lower your fert's risk of insulinoma.

- **Lymphosarcoma.** Symptoms of this condition are not always immediately evident, but may include lethargy, weight loss and difficulty breathing. This cancer attacks the lymphatic system, and is most likely to occur in a fuzzy with a weakened immune system. Chemotherapy is a treatment option which you should discuss with your veterinarian.

- **Skin tumors.** There are several types of skin tumors that are common to ferrets including mast cell tumors, sebaceous tumors and basal cell tumors. These tumors are, more often than not, benign. It is possible for them to get infected or cause your fuzzball some discomfort so discuss having them removed with your vet.

Cardiomyopathy

Cardiomyopathy is a heart disease in which the lining of a ferret's heart muscle thins or thickens, eventually killing the heart muscle all together. Without the muscle power behind it, the heart loses its ability to work effectively.

Symptoms of this disease include a hacking cough, listlessness, coughing and difficulty breathing. Your fuzzy may develop a pot-belly due to the accumulation of fluid in his stomach.

Depending on the extent of the damage to the heart, it's possible to manage this condition with medication, a change in diet, and reduced activity. With proper care, your ferret may have another two years left in him.

Epizootic Catarrhal Enteritis

This disease is caused by a coronavirus, and it is transmitted very easily between ferrets. It is usually spread when a new ferret is introduced into the home or into a shelter environment, which is one of the reasons you are encouraged to keep new ferts quarantined for at least a week before introducing him to your other fuzzies.

The illness is marked by severe irritation in a fert's intestinal tract and causes slimy green diarrhea with an extremely foul odor. Older ferrets are usually more seriously affected than youngsters.

Left untreated, this condition can be fatal. Because this disease affects the absorption of nutrients, fuzzies are at serious risk from dehydration and malnutrition. Treatment of this illness includes a high calorie dietary supplement and IV fluids.

Gastric Ulcers

Like humans, ferrets are susceptible to ulcers. Bacteria is one cause of ulcers, and some can develop in ferts who are under stress. Stressors include things like adding a new ferret, moving, a cage-mate dying, and anything else that disturbs your fuzzy. Some clues that your ferret is suffering from a gastric ulcer are that he will be producing tarry, black stools and you may notice him grinding his teeth.

As with humans, ulcers can cause your fert a great deal of abdominal pain and discomfort. Left untreated, ulcers can be fatal.

Aleutian Mink Disease Virus

This viral disease is a type of parvovirus, and it most often affects the kidneys and liver.

Other than that there isn't too much known about it. It's believed that there are several different strains of this virus, and the severity of the illness depends on which strain is affecting the ferret. Transmission occurs through the exchange of bodily fluids, the air and surfaces that have been contaminated by the disease. Symptoms include chronic weight loss, tremors, tarry stools, and weakness.

Chapter 13: What to Expect When You're Expecting Ferrets

You've absolutely fallen in love with your fur kids, and now you'd love to have the pitter pat of even more little paws running through the house. But is becoming a breeder really right for you?

Let's examine your reasons for thinking of breeding your ferrets. Take plenty of time to consider the following questions...

- **Are you hoping to make some extra money breeding ferrets?** If so, you may be disappointed. It takes money to properly care for your jills, hobs and their kits. In addition to more food, toys and litter, you'll need appropriate cages for everyone keeping in mind that nursing mothers and rutting males will need their own personal space. The ferts you breed will need full physicals, as well as regular vaccinations. Their kits will need to get their initial vaccinations while under your care. All of these things cost money. Reputable breeders are usually not making a profit. They are doing it because they truly love these creatures.

- **Do you have the time?** Think about all of the exercise and playtime one ferret needs. Now multiply that by the number of ferrets and kits you plan to have at any given time. You'll also need time to take your fur kids and their babies back and forth for vet visits and to spend talking to potential buyers to answer all of their questions and ensure that your kits will be placed in appropriate homes.

- **Do all of the ferrets you are planning on breeding have sound temperaments and clean bills of health?** It would be irresponsible to breed animals with serious health conditions or aggressive temperaments that they could pass on to their offspring. Are you prepared to spay or neuter ferrets that are not appropriate for breeding? Are you willing to take on the care of them for the rest of their lives if you can't find them suitable homes?

- **Are you prepared to take the time and effort needed to screen potential buyers?** There is more to selling your kits than handing them over to anyone willing to plunk down the money. As much time, money and emotion that you'll be investing in your ferts, you won't want them to go home with just anyone. You'll want to carefully screen anyone interested in buying them to make sure that they can give them the best possible care.

- **Are you prepared for when things don't go as planned?** Sometimes mothers eat their young or refuse to nurse them. Sometimes kits die or are born with serious health conditions. Buyers decide it's not working out and want to return the ferret to you, or worse, dump the ferret outside or at the nearest shelter. Do you have plan for all of these contingencies?

- **Do you know your state's laws regarding breeding ferrets?** Check into any possible permits or licenses you may need.

As you can see from these questions, breeding ferrets is not something to be jumped into lightly. It involves a large commitment from you and a true love for ferrets. Only after giving long and hard thought to everything involved in breeding should you make the decision to breed your fuzzies.

The following information on breeding your ferts is meant to give you a general idea of what to expect. It does not cover every possible complication and nuance of creating a successful breeding program. It is intended to give you more information to help guide you in making the decision to breed. You are urged to do much more intensive research if, after reading this chapter, you still feel like breeding is for you.

Mating Your Ferts

Unaltered males usually go into rut between December and July. During this time they may not be the most pleasant creatures to share your life with. They tend to smell more than usual, and they can become quite aggressive toward other male ferrets, your other pets, and you.

They also have the tendency to mount any object they can get their paws around. They should definitely be given their own bachelor pad during this time.

The female goes into season between March and August. She will stay in heat until she is bred. If you aren't planning on breeding her during this heat cycle, she will need a visit to the veterinarian for a hormone injection to bring her out of heat. Most breeders only breed a female once or twice a season. The best time to mate your ferts is about two weeks after the female goes into heat.

 Each fuzzy's individual cycle may differ a little from the ones mentioned above. Keep a close eye on your ferts to keep track of their cycles. Males who are ready for mating usually have an off-white undercoat. Females' genitals noticeably swell.

When you are sure the time is right, you can bring the female to the male's bachelor pad. Plan on supervising for at least a little while to make sure that things are going to progress the way they're supposed to.

Believe it or not, if the male bites the female's neck and pulls her around his cage, and then proceeds to mate with her for several hours, things are going as they are supposed to. The neck biting and the physical act of mating cause the female's eggs to be released so it is a vital part of the mating ritual.

Along with the neck biting there may be a little bit of blood, but more than that is not usual mating behavior. If this is the case, you may need to separate the pair.

Once your pair has begun to mate, do not separate them. They are physically hooked together until the male has finished. Pulling them apart can physically harm the fuzzies.

Plan on keeping the pair together for a couple of days.

The Pregnant Female

If the mating has been successful, you should be able to feel the kits in mom's belly within a few weeks. The jill will need to take in more calories throughout the pregnancy and while she is nursing her kits. Some extra dietary supplements or other high protein treats, such as chicken, beef or eggs, in addition to your fuzzball's regular diet, are a great way to give your female the extra protein and fat she needs to sustain her growing kits.

As the time of the kits' birth draws closer, mom must be given her own personal space. This spot should include something that can be used as a nest, such as a cat litter box, and extra bedding. If you are using your ferret's regular cage, you may need to add some sort of guard around the bars at the bottom to keep kits from slipping through the bars of the cage.

As with humans, a jill's nesting instinct kicks in as she gets closer to the birth of her babies. She'll fluff up the nesting material, and may even add tufts of her own fur, to keep her kits as warm and comfortable as possible.

 Other pets, kids and anything else that can cause loud disruptions should be kept away from mom as the time draws close for the birth.

Mom should be ready to give birth about forty-two days after being bred.

Arrival of the Babies

Plan to keep watch from a discreet distance once mom goes into labor. Once she starts giving birth, labor is usually completed in three or four hours, depending on the size of her litter.

Some things you should watch for:

- **Kits getting stuck in the birth canal.** This can cause a lot of trouble. Mom will be in pain and unable to tend to the kits who have already been born, putting them in jeopardy, and the kit in the birth canal can die.

- **Too many umbilical cords at one time.** If the birth of each kit comes close together, mom may have trouble cutting each cord before it becomes mixed up with the others. In this case, you may need to shorten the umbilical cords to make mom's job easier. Do this as quickly, quietly and unobtrusively as possible.

- **Kits stuck in the placental sack.** Help them to get free of the sack if needed, and then allow mom to take over care of the kit.

 Many breeders give their vet a call at the onset of labor so they can be ready in case of emergency. If there is any doubt as to the health and well-being of mom and babies, call your veterinarian immediately. Waiting too long can mean the difference between life and death.

The Babies Are Here... Now What?

Once the babies have been safely delivered, you should make every effort to keep things quiet for the first few days to allow mom and babies to get comfortable with one another. You should be the only person allowed in the room and only to clean the cage and feed mom. Mom will usually eat the placenta, but you may need to do a little extra cleaning after the birth. Give mom and kits a day or so, though, before you make this effort.

 Mother ferts who have too much activity, noise or other disturbances around after the birth have been known to eat their young.

There are some things you can do to make sure that the first days of the kits' lives go smoothly...

- Give mom some extra tempting food to stimulate her to eat. Hunger may keep her from nursing right away.

- Moms will reject a kit if he isn't warm. If one gets separated from mom, warm him up before putting him back near her.

- Keep an eye on the kits to make sure they are gaining weight. A failure to thrive may mean that mom isn't producing enough milk or having trouble nursing. If this is the case, you may need to put the kits in with another lactating female to ensure that they are getting adequate nutrition, and bring mom to the veterinarian for a health check.

 Many breeders breed more than one female at a time. This ensures that there is more than one lactating female available to feed kits in case one of the mothers has some trouble.

By the time ferrets reach six weeks of age, they're active and ready to start exploring the world. It's your job to make sure that they have a positive view of the world. Starting around this time, kits should be handled a great deal to socialize them to people.

By eight weeks of age they'll be ready for regular ferret kibble (or the raw food diet). You may start trying to place them in their forever homes at this point, although some breeders prefer to wait until they're twelve weeks or older. It's important that you wait until your kits are at least eight weeks old to remove them from their mother and siblings.

They're Ready to Go Home... Now What?

When it comes time to send your ferts to their new homes, you can advertise by word of mouth, classified ads, a ferret club or the internet. No matter how people find you, you need to take special care in placing your kits. Ask as many questions as you need to in order to feel satisfied with your kits' new families.

 No matter how thorough you are in your screening process, a situation will crop up every now and then where a ferret will need to be returned to you or you will find out that all is not well in the home in which you placed him. It happens to every breeder at one time or another. So it's important you create a contract that must be signed before someone can purchase one of your fuzzies. In this contract, include stipulations about the type of care the ferret must be given and what the purchaser should do if they find themselves in a situation in which they are no longer able to care for the ferret.

Some questions you must ask potential buyers to make sure you kits won't be put into abusive homes include:

- **Where do you live?** Sounds simple, but because ferrets are illegal in some places, it's important that someone buying one of your ferts doesn't live in one of these places.

- **Have you had pets before, and if so, what happened to them?** The best predictor for the type of care they'll give your kit is their history of pet ownership. Ask permission to speak to their veterinarian to make sure they've always given their pets routine veterinary care. Ask for personal references who can attest to the fact that they are good pet owners.

- **Where do you plan to house your ferret?**

- **What are your plans for giving your ferret exercise?**

- **Are you aware of the expenses associated with owning a ferret?** For example, a lot of people fail to budget for vet bills, thinking they're one-time costs and don't matter... when in fact they're significant expenses that all ferret owners must face eventually.

The time you spend talking to potential families for your kits should give you ample time to do some educating. Many people purchasing ferrets are going to be first time ferret owners just as you once were. Take the time to make sure they are aware of the ups and downs of sharing their lives with an animal as unique, inquisitive and lively as a ferret.

Chapter 14: Some Final Dook

There is one thing for certain when you make the decision to share your life with a ferret -- things will never be dull! Fuzzies are wonderful creatures who can amuse you for hours with their intelligence and their silly cavorting. Bringing one (or more) into your home can mean many years shared with a lively companion.

Here are some of the finer points of living with a ferret:

- Just like people, all ferrets are unique individuals. However, there are some factors such as age, sex, and colorations which can help you choose the right fuzzy for your family (more on this in Chapter 3).

- Ferrets are not meant to live in cages like hamsters or guinea pigs. A nice roomy cage is fine for when he can't be supervised, but to live a happy and healthy life your ferret needs to get plenty of time outside of his cage playing and socializing with you (see Chapters 8 & 9 for more on your ferret's housing and exercise requirements).

- If you don't plan on breeding your ferrets, it's important that you have them altered. Once an unspayed female goes into heat, she stays in heat until she's bred. Without mating or a hormone injection to bring her out of heat, a female can develop a condition which can lead to death.

Unneutered males can become aggressive and difficult to live with when they're in rut (see Chapter 3 to learn more about the pros and cons of altering your fuzzy).

- Your fuzzy's good health starts with a healthy FFAT diet which should contain fat, low fiber, animal protein and taurine. Plant matter is indigestible to ferts so it should only be given as treats in small quantities (Chapter 7 covers all you need to know about feeding your fert).

- If you have ferrets and children in the house, make sure they are always supervised when they're together. Children have a tendency to make lots of noise, squeeze ferts too tightly and startle fuzzies with their movements. It's important that you never allow your children to put your fuzzy into a position to defend himself (Chapter 6 goes into more detail on living with kids and ferts).

- It's important to establish rules for your ferret from the time you bring him home. Using positive training methods, you can train your fert not to nip, to use his litter box, and to do tricks just for fun (more on training your fuzzball in Chapters 9 & 10).

- Your ferret needs regular veterinary care including a physical and yearly vaccinations. Find a veterinarian who specializes in the care of ferrets (see Chapter 11 & 12 for more on your fert's health).

- Breeding is not for everyone. Do some research and ask yourself some serious questions before making the decision to commit to such a huge undertaking (for more on breeding your fuzzies, see Chapter 13).

Living with a ferret is not for everyone. If you haven't opened your home to a ferret yet, hopefully you will take the preceding chapters into consideration before deciding whether or not a fuzzy is right for you. Ferrets have many good points – they're fun-loving, intelligent, quiet, and full of mischief. They also have a few habits that not everyone can appreciate -- they like to dig, chew, steal your things and they can be messy. They need your time, attention and love.

If you already have a ferret, hopefully you've learned a few things here that will help make living with your ferret an even more enjoyable experience.

Whether you already share your home with ferrets or are just thinking of getting a fuzzball, you have probably gained new appreciation and insight into these special creatures. If you've fallen in love with the lively antics, chuckling laughter, and joyful dances of these animals, join the club. Most people who add fuzzies to their families find themselves charmed and captivated for years to come.

Best wishes for you and your fuzzy,

Colin Patterson

Colin Patterson
Athens, GA USA
September 1, 2006

RESOURCES

Books and Magazines

Amazing Ferret Secrets

By Danielle Wexler

> Valuable guide containing, among other things, a guide to building your own ferret house and a recipe book of food you can prepare for your ferrets. You can get to Danielle's site by going to http://findoutaboutferrets.com/amazingsecrets

Ferrets for Dummies (Wiley Publishing, Inc., 2000)

By Kim Schilling

> Comprehensive, informative guide to ferrets and their care. Learn more at http://findoutaboutferrets.com/ferretsfordummies

The Simple Guide to Ferrets (T.F.H. Publications, Inc., 2003)

By Bobbye Land

> Good book which touches on all things ferret. Learn more at http://findoutaboutferrets.com/simpleguide

The Ferret: An Owner's Guide to a Happy Healthy Pet (Howell Book House, 1996)

By Mary R. Shefferman

> Great book for the first time owner. Contains helpful information on ferret care and health. Learn more at http://findoutaboutferrets.com/happyhealthy

<u>Training Your Pet Ferret</u> (Barron's Educational Series, Inc., 1997)

By Gerry Bucsis and Barbara Somerville

> ➤ Has some good tips on training your ferret, as long as you keep in mind that not every solution works on every fert. Learn more at <u>http://findoutaboutferrets.com/training</u>

<u>How To Roar: Pet Loss Grief Recovery</u> (Spring Water Publishing, 2005)

By Robin Jean Brown

> ➤ If you're suffering from the sadness of the death of your ferret, this warm, helpful combination book/workbook will take you through the stages of grief so that you can come out at the end with a deeper understanding and appreciation of what your fuzzy meant to you. Also available in ebook form for instant download at <u>http://petlossguide.com</u>

Modern Ferret

P.O. Box 1007

Smithtown, NY 11787

Email: mary@modernferret.com, ferrets@modernferret.com

Website: <u>www.modernferret.com</u>

> ➤ Bi-monthly magazine created by husband and wife ferret owners to bring you all you need to know about caring for your fuzzy.

Organizations

The American Ferret Association, Inc.

PMB 255

626-C Admiral Dr.

Annapolis, MD 21401

Phone: 1-888-FERRET1

Website: http://www.ferret.org

> ➢ This organization is dedicated to promoting the domestic ferret as a companion animal. They offer a variety of services from educational programs to breeder and shelter referrals. They also provide local veterinary referrals.

National Association of Professional Pet Sitters (NAPPS)

15000 Commerce Parkway, Suite C

Mount Laurel, NJ 08054

Phone: 856-439-0324

Email: napps@ahint.com

Website: http://www.petsitters.org

> ➢ Provides pet sitter referrals, as well as education and networking opportunities for pet sitters.

American Society for the Prevention of Cruelty to Animals (ASPCA)

424 E. 92nd Street

New York, NY 10128-6804

Phone: 212-876-7700

Website: http://www.aspca.org

> ➢ Non-profit organization devoted to animal welfare. Website contains a great deal of information on pet care, emergency preparedness, and other helpful tips.

The Humane Society of the United States

2100 L Street, NW

Washington, DC 20037

202-452-1100

Website: http://www.hsus.org

> This organization promotes the protection of all animals through education, legislation, disaster assistance, and other campaigns. Their website is loaded with information on the basics of ferret care, as well as other helpful tips.

Websites

http://www.petfinder.com

> Website devoted to helping you meet your fuzzy match. This site contains listings of a variety of companion animals (including ferrets) available for adoption all over the country.

1-800-PetMeds

> A lot of people save money by finding out from their vet what medication their ferret needs, then ordering it from 1800PetMeds. Learn more at http://findoutaboutferrets.com/petmeds

The Ferret Store

> Great place to go for all of your fuzzy's needs. They offer cages, toys, litter pans, and other accessories. The website also offers a live chat Monday through Friday which allows you to connect immediately to their in-house ferret expert. Learn more at http://findoutaboutferrets.com/ferretstore

http://www.veterinarypartner.com

> Provides information on health, behavior, drugs and more on a variety of animals, including ferts.

Wysong

> Sellers of the Archetype diet, a raw food diet made with ferrets' special nutritional needs in mind. Learn more at http://findoutaboutferrets.com/wysong

http://www.veterinarypartner.com

About the Author

Born and raised in New England, Colin Patterson has been involved with small animal rescue and has been a small animal trainer, breeder and consultant for almost three decades.

He and his wife split time between Boston, Massachusetts and Athens, GA and are owned by 5 ferrets, 17 pet rats, 5 gerbils, 2 rabbits, 12 guinea pigs, 2 hamsters, 1 chinchilla and 4 pet mice.

Colin has also written a guide to pet rats called <u>Pet Rats: How to Easily Train and Care For Your Ratties...To Have a Happy Life Together</u> which is at <u>http://petratguide.com</u>

CPSIA information can be obtained
at www.ICGtesting.com
Printed in the USA
LVHW060329030419
612795LV00004B/259/P

9 781847 285232